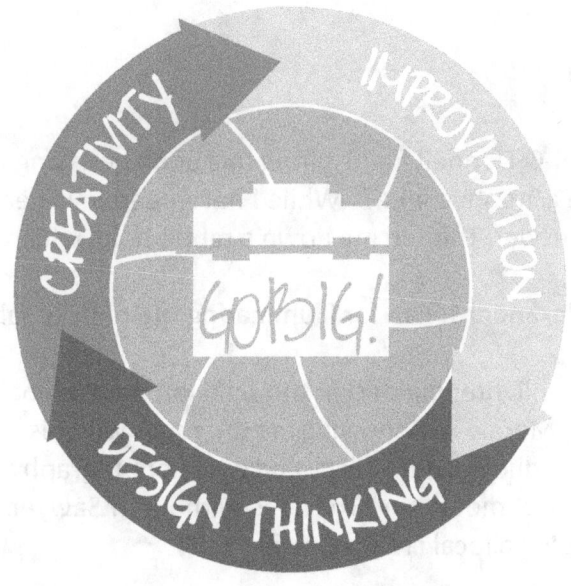

TOOLKIT

Create Simply.
Simply Create.

Chris Mumford

Acknowledgements

I would like to thank Randee Haven-O'Donnell for inspiring this book by asking the innocent question, "What happens if someone doesn't have a creative idea?" While I have been involved in design-related businesses for a long time, I did not have an answer. This led me down a rabbit hole, which is how the book was created.

I am grateful to my design guru Alexander Julian for illuminating the path to fabulous design.

I appreciate Haig Khachatoorian's enlightening design thoughts on how to soar with the condors and dance with ants. Special thanks to Manny Morales for showing me the ropes with his right brain-left, brain brilliance. I am grateful to James Slade for introducing me to black and white photography, my first medium of creativity. I am so appreciative for my insightful mountain bike rides with Keith Sawyer. Thanks to Judith Cone's and Michelle Bola's support in developing a local creative community.

Copyright 2014 by Chris Mumford

All rights reserved. No part of this book shall be reproduced, stored in a retrieval system or transmitted by any means, electronic, mechanical, photocopying, recording or otherwise, without written permission of the publisher/author. Request to the author should be addressed to joe@joestartup.com.

Limit of Liability/disclaimer of Warranty: While the publisher and author have used their best efforts in preparing this book, they make no representations or warranties with respect to the accuracy or completeness of the contents of this book and specifically disclaim any implied warranties of merchantability or fitness for a particular
purpose. The advice and strategies contained herein may not be suitable for your situation. You should consult with a professional where appropriate. Neither the publisher nor author shall be liable for any loss of profit or any other commercial damages, including but not limited to special, incidental, consequential, or other damages.

Library of Congress Cataloging-in-Publication Data: Pending

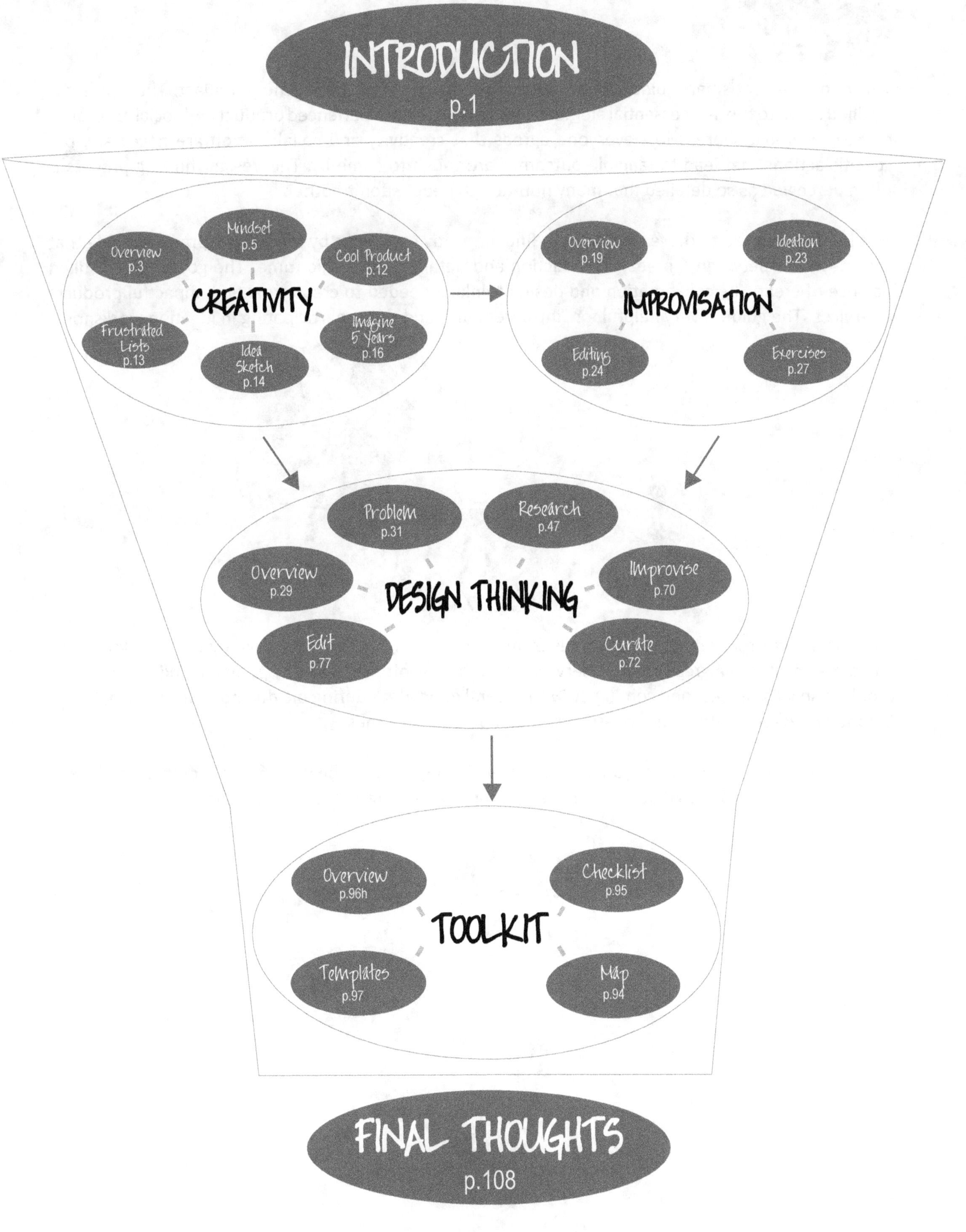
INTRODUCTION
p.1
Overview
p.3
Mindset
p.5
Cool Product
p.12
CREATIVITY
Frustrated Lists
p.13
Idea Sketch
p.14
Imagine 5 Years
p.16
Overview
p.19
Ideation
p.23
IMPROVISATION
Editing
p.24
Exercises
p.27
Problem
p.31
Research
p.47
Overview
p.29
DESIGN THINKING
Improvise
p.70
Edit
p.77
Curate
p.72
Overview
p.96h
Checklist
p.95
TOOLKIT
Templates
p.97
Map
p.94
FINAL THOUGHTS
p.108

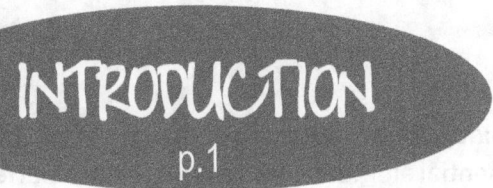

Introduction

This book is street smart-guide written for people that want to make a huge impact. The content is distilled down to the most essential elements, namely what an experienced product and social enterprise developer would share. Most everyone agrees that creativity and collaboration are necessary, but specific actions that lead to tangible outcomes are tough to come by. The design thinking process is often perceived as so detailed that many non-design people don't bother.

This book is devoted to those who want to find innovative solutions by following a practical guide that is somewhere between a breezy introduction and detailed, academic tome. The goal is the distilled balance of creativity, collaboration and design thinking needed to create real and impactful products a services. The guide is very helpful for "intrapreneurs" and those participating in ideation workshops.

There is a myth that great design comes from a single designer who is struck by one fabulous idea and develops it into a great product/service. The reality is often a group of people working through a problem-solving process and coming up with several good ideas during playful moments of "what-ifs.". Creativity is directed through process to create fabulous outcomes.

The key approach is open-minded discovery: considering the possibilities of what could be and then narrowing those down to what will work best, given real constraints and time limits.

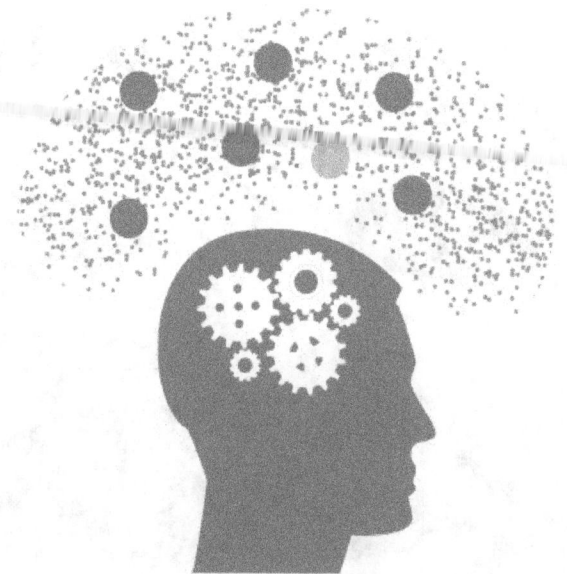

Most successful product developers will readily admit that their initial assumptions about the user, problem and solution are very different than those used in the final product/service. Many entrepreneurs think they know exactly what the customer wants without actually validating with customers, often with disastrous results. As a result, the ideal design mindset is one of discovery, knowing that many things will change through the process.

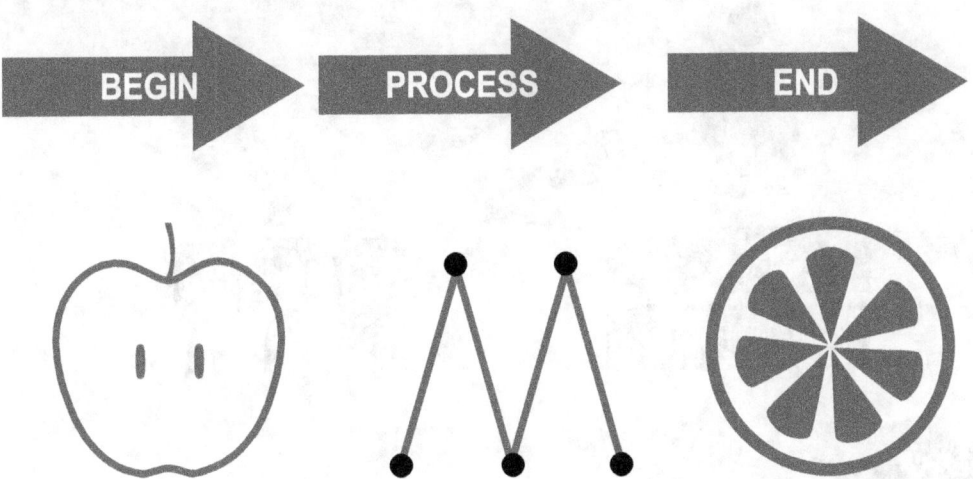

This book is broken down into four sections: Creativity, Improvisation, Design Thinking and the Toolkit. Creativity provides the spark, Improvisation grows the fire, and Design Thinking channels the heat. The Toolkit puts it all together in a step-by-step plan. The synergy of the Creative Mindset, Improvisation and Design Thinking is what differentiates this book from others.

In Creativity, we develop the creative mindset through actions to promote divergent thinking. Creativity must be trained daily like a muscle to produce effective outcomes. Creativity is foundational to design and improvisation.

In Improvisation, we borrow heavily from comedy improv. Well-done improvisation and innovation both require great team chemistry. A playful, productive environment is created by developing explicit engagement rules, a no-fail environment and authentic relationships. Team chemistry and empathy supercharges Design Thinking.

In Design Thinking, we explore the step-by-step process of channeling creativity. The process of discovery through telling the product/service story is important.

In Toolkit, the process is formatted into an easy-to-reuse checklist and plan for individuals and groups.

The book will encourage you to move back and forth from the big picture to the essential details. Soar with condors and dance with ants. In the end, great design comes from developing your own creativity, developing authentic relationships and discovering the product/service story through design thinking.

There are three examples used throughout the book to better understand the execution:

1. A app who helps parents find playmates for their children and other compatible parents.
2. A parent advocate which helps low wealth parents with kids aged 0-6 learn best parenting practices.
3. A bike desk for professionals wanting to get healthy while working.

Creativity

Overview

Creativity requires first mastering and transcending traditional ideas, rules, patterns and relationships, and second realizing a new idea that was both intended and received to be uniquely valuable by one's peers.

Mastering an area of knowledge, or domain, is critical to creativity. Musicians must learn and perform the work of great composers who came before them; professional basketball shooting guards must be able to hit every shot from any spot on court.

Creativity is often expressed in incremental, namely small improvements, and rarely through breakthroughs, or by overcoming a difficult obstacle. Incremental outcomes are most common because most things have been done before.

Incremental improvements most often happen when there is a twist, or an unexpected positive surprise, to a familiar pattern. Current pop music is often a remix or mashup of songs past. Most product design is a balance of improving functionality and refreshing design lines from the past.

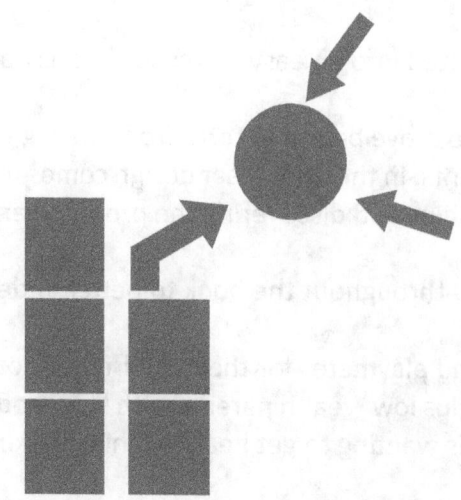

When breakthrough improvements do happen, they are often the results of either combining massive data gathering with deductive reasoning in new areas, or applying patterns from one domain to new domains. To illustrate, cancer treatments are most often incremental improvements, while Amazon and eBay breakthrough improvements.

While convergent thinking, or logic, can be helpful for realizing new ideas, divergent thinking is often the greatest source of unique ideas. Divergent thinking is a process of developing new ideas by exploring many different possible solutions. In simple terms, divergent thinking would encourage you to drive home several different ways to see if one is better. Perhaps routes and traffic patterns have changed over time. The idea is to regularly challenge assumptions by breaking patterns to see if there is a better pattern. Albert Einstein is credited with saying "creativity is seeing what everyone else has seen, and thinking what no one else has thought."

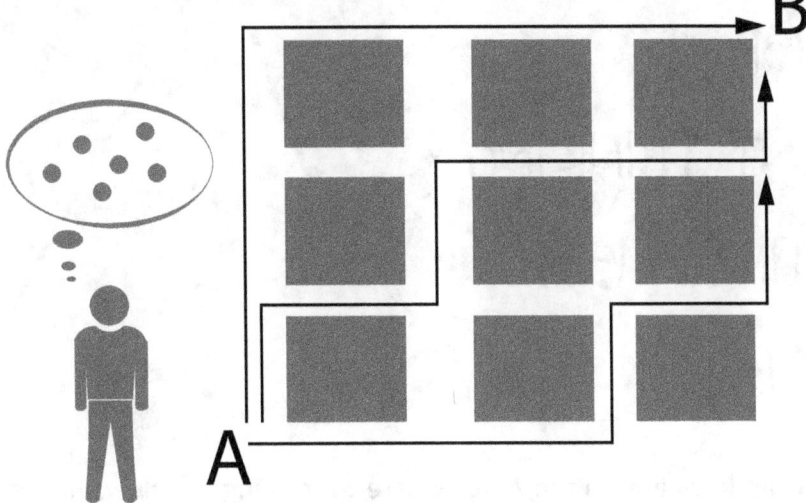

The key question is how to develop your divergent thinking skills. How do we encourage you to connect the dots in all the possible ways and then choose the best way?

Most people say they are not creative. Most 7-year-olds are great at divergent thinking. Somehow our education system has greatly promoted logic at the expense of divergent thinking. Creativity happens in the uncomfortable space at the edge of the known and unknown; go different routes.

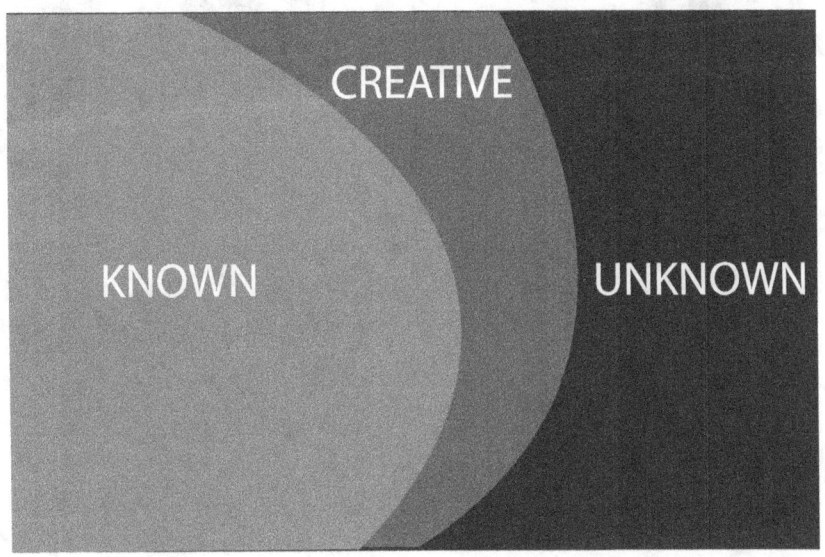

Mindset

A. The creative mindset is about developing habits which promote domain expertise, divergent thinking, new stimulus and having regular practice. The unique ability to connect the dots needs to be rediscovered. Like an unused muscle, the creative mindset needs to be nurtured and strengthened daily.

CREATIVE MINDSET =
EXPERTISE +
DIVERGENT THINKING +
NEW STIMULUS +
PRACTICE

B. We often hear how athletes are "in the zone" where everything just flows naturally. For artists and writers, it seems ideas present themselves almost as gifts, that is, with little effort. The reality is that getting "in the zone" usually happens when there is a mindset, a structure, and lots of practice.

IN THE ZONE

C. Even improvisational comedy follows rules to facilitate the creation of funny scenes. In short, we need a framework and the right mindset to produce creative outcomes. A few exercises will help.

Domain expertise
1. Block out 20 minutes a day to keep updated on the most recent developments in your field and those adjacent. People are often so busy that they don't have time to keep up. Make it a top priority whether you are a research scientist or a rapper.

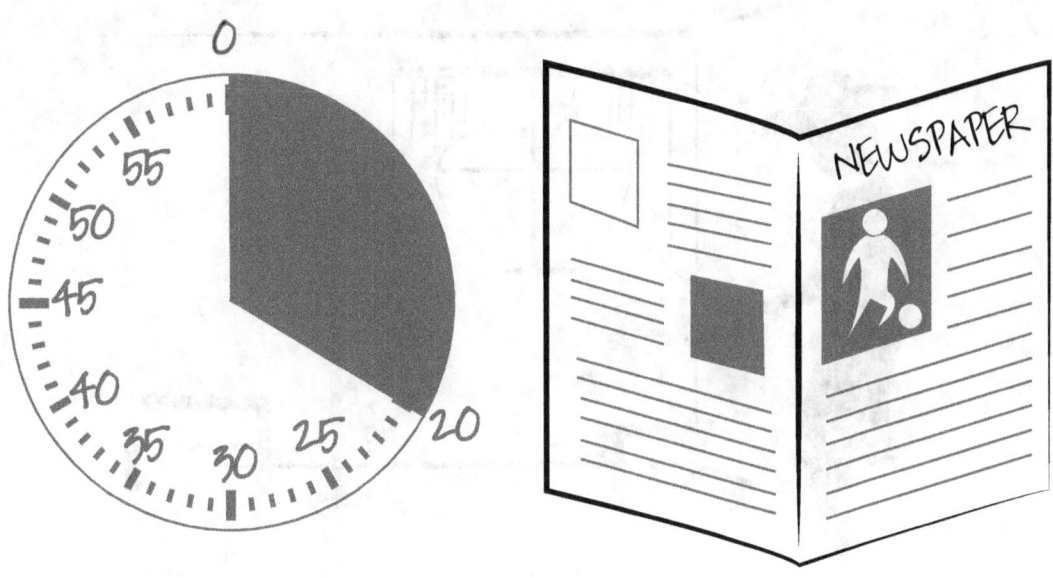

Divergent thinking
1. Consider your daily habits and patterns: How you get ready for work/school? How you get to work/school? Constantly think of all the options. Break some habits by trying something new. Test them. Instill this inclination in your normal thought process. Always ask "is there a way to do this better?"

New Stimulus

1. Imagine that you are a spy and that you have to memorize all the details of a room. What is the paint color? What is the trim like? Where is the light coming from? In this exercise, focus on the present moment.

2. Every day take 20 minutes to look for inspiration online or offline. Consider breakfast, lunch or a coffee break. Interesting design or cool products can help you define what you want. Understand how innovation is happening in other areas and ask yourself how they could apply to your area of expertise.

3. Make a "what makes me frustrated" list. Think about badly solved or unsolved problems at home, work, or elsewhere. What solutions—products or services—could you offer to deal with these problems? For example, city dwellers desperately wanted to use cars for errands or short trips. The solution provided was short-term rental cars parked in convenient city locations. List other people's frustrations.

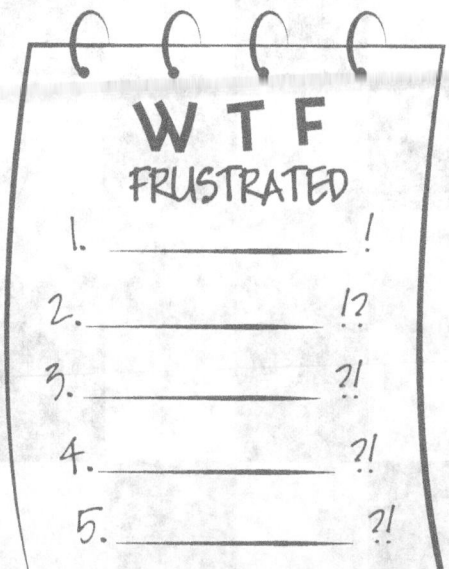

4. If you are drawing a blank, create an idea sketch. Write out and circle the user or idea in the middle of the page. Surround the user/idea with assumptions, constraints or stakeholders to understand the relationship of things. See more details below.

Practice Time

1. Set aside creative time every day. It could be as little as 15 minutes to as much as several hours. Review your inspiration journal.

A. Ask the question, "What if…" to promote divergent thinking.
B. Once you have started to connect the dots and have a direction, then ask, "If this is the case, then what?" to promote convergent thinking.

CREATIVE TIME

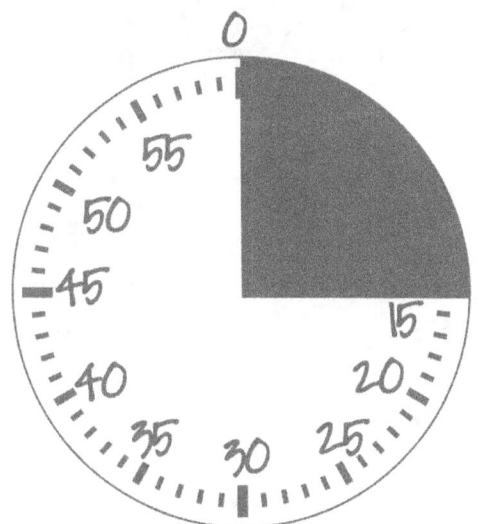
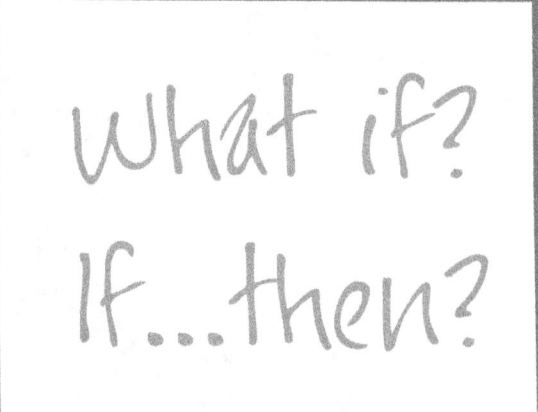

2. The first time will seem hard, but like a muscle, creativity will come stronger if you are consistent. Establishing a new pattern takes time. Create a regular ritual for your creative sessions the same way a free-throw shooter uses the same ritual before each shot. Experiment with what works – time limits, frequent breaks, physical movement – until you create your own creative zone. Be mindful of the environment you require to be creative and make it.

— TIME
— RITUAL
— MOVEMENT
— ENVIRONMENT

3. Keep a hobby that allows your mind to wander — a type of activity that allows the brain to process life's details. Ideally, observe your thoughts without forming attachments or feelings. The longer the activity, (such as an hour or more),, the better as the best ideas tend to come after processing the daily grind.

4. Try an exercise or a hobby that encourages you to focus on the present moment and nothing else. Sometimes the mind needs to process ideas in the background while attention is on something else.

5. Try the "Imagine in 5 years..." exercise. Imagine that you are going up an elevator in 5 years and others around you are talking about your idea or project. How would they describe it in short, specific phrases? Write these ideas down on paper or on a whiteboard. This exercise will give you a glimpse of what could be.

A. Don't pressure yourself to come up with the one great idea. Most successful ideas are mash-ups of previous ideas. Pablo Picasso said "good artists copy, great artists steal." The iPhone is literally a mash-up of a phone, a music player, and computer apps.

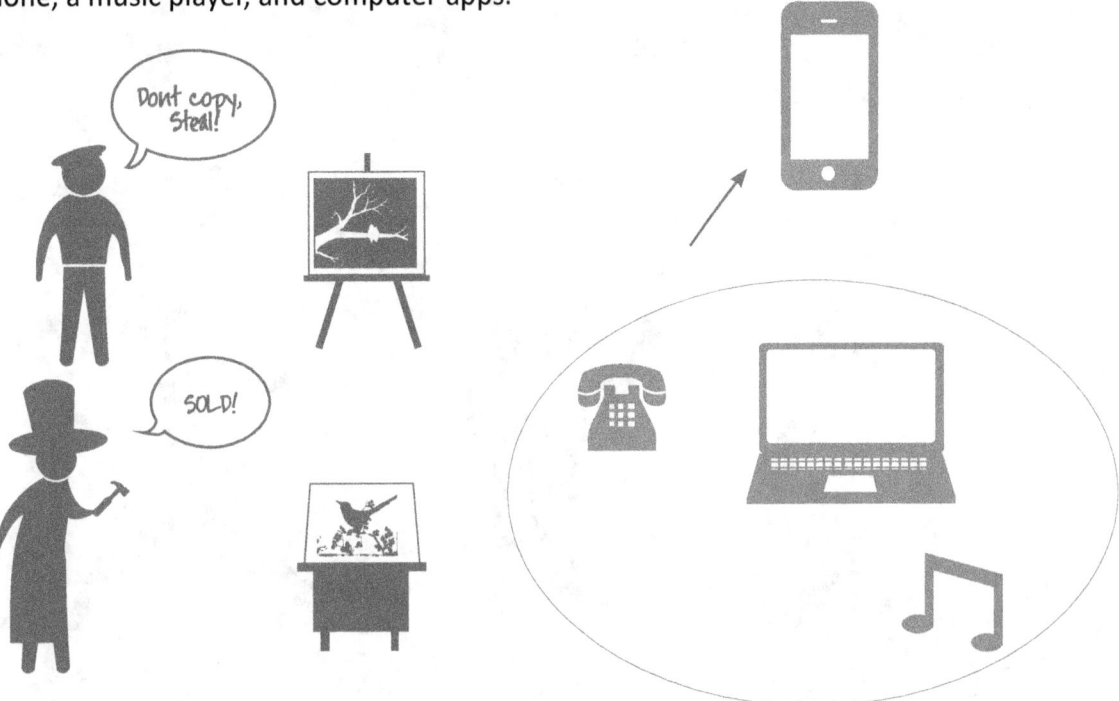

B. eBay is an auction (a centuries old idea) applied online. In fact, many great concepts are ideas from one field applied to another. So remix ideas from one part of life and apply them to another.

C. During practice time, practice divergent thinking (what if?) to generate new ideas. Then, use convergent (logic) thinking (if...then...) – to turn those ideas into practical solutions.

D. Doing these exercises regularly will help you get in the creative zone. Many ideas will present themselves to you. Be willing to entertain a number of bad ideas to come up with a few good ideas. Put yourself out there, and believe that the process will ultimately yield good results.

Cool Products and Services Journal

A. Don't pressure yourself to come up with the one great idea. Most successful ideas are mash-ups of previous ideas. Pablo Picasso said "good artists copy, great artists steal." The iPhone is literally a mash-up of a phone, a music player, and computer apps.

Cool Products & Services	
What	Website

# What Makes Me Frustrated List

Think about badly solved or unsolved problems at home, work, or elsewhere. What solutions—products or services—could you offer to deal with these problems?

What Makes Me Frustrated List

Image Sketching

In a group or as an individual, draw out an idea sketch with the user or idea in the middle. Add all the possible stakeholders, constraints and assumptions. On the lower left hand corner, write out open questions in abbreviated form. On the lower right hand corner, scribble essential details in abbreviated form. Refine as needed.

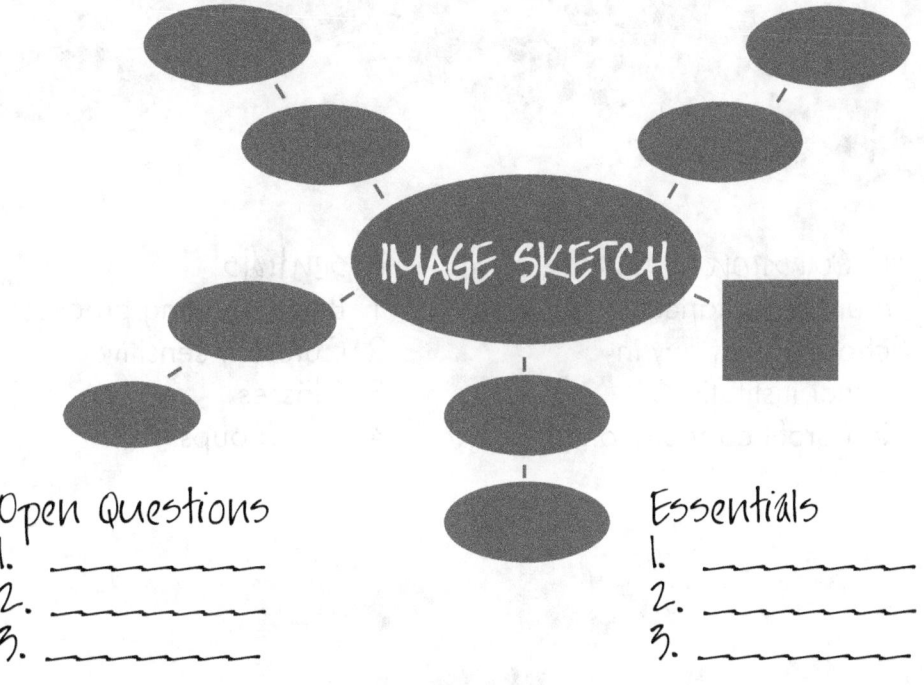

Open Questions
1. _____
2. _____
3. _____

Essentials
1. _____
2. _____
3. _____

EXAMPLES

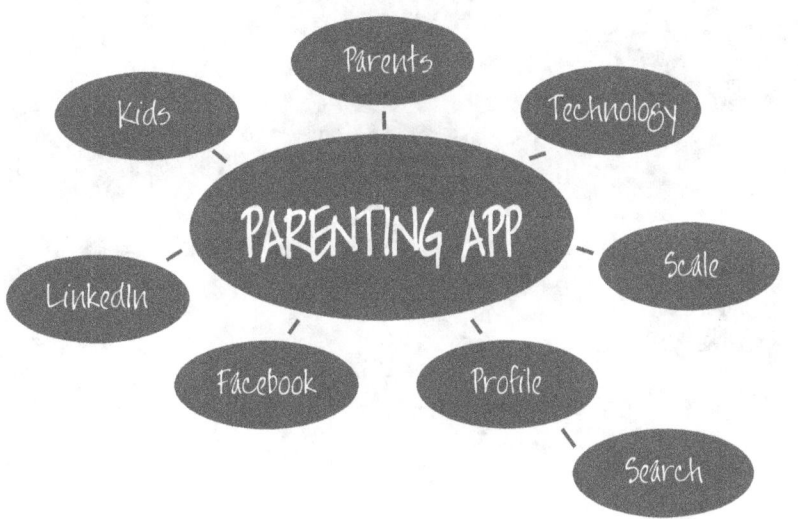

Open Question
1. Parent adoption
2. App design
3. Kids product company needs

Essentials
1. LinkedIn for kids and parents
2. Profile building easy
3. Search with filters

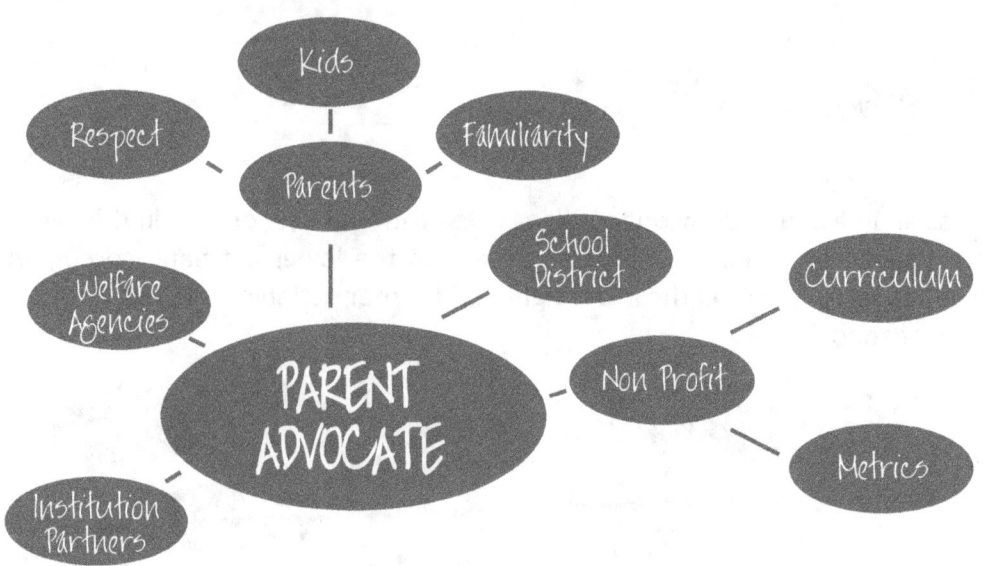

Open Question
1. Parent acceptance
2. School district buy in
3. Partner institutions
4. Non profit cooperation

Essentials
1. Best parenting practices
2. Cuturally sensitive
3. Classes
4. Play groups

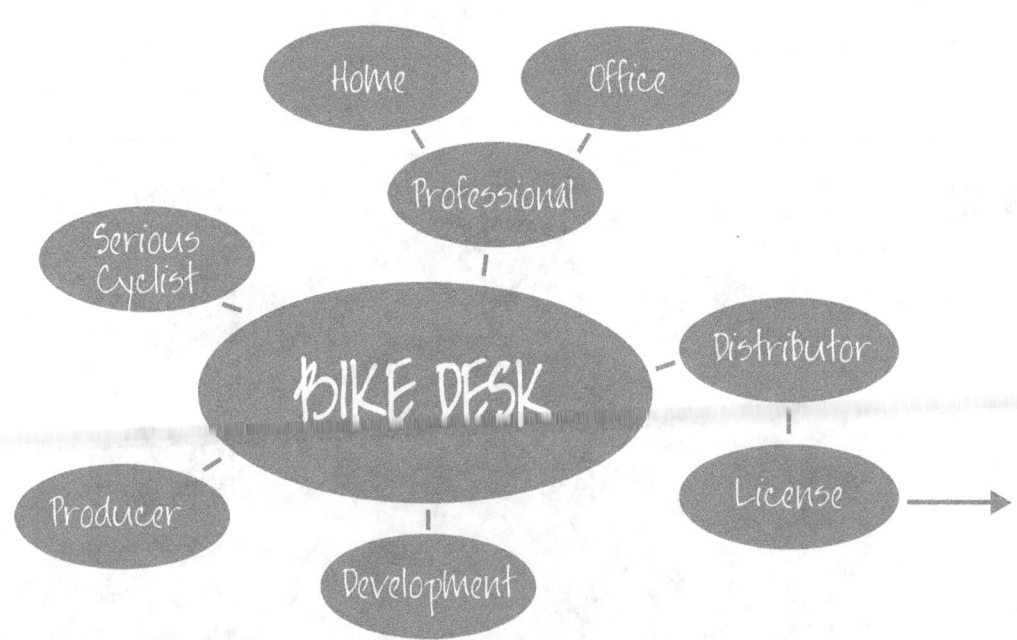

Open Question
1. Include cycle
2. Licensing
3. Target audience

Essentials
1. Desk with indoor cycling

Imagine in 5 Years

Imagine that you are going up an elevator in 5 years and others around you are talking about your idea or project. How would they describe it in short phrases? Write these ideas down on paper or on a whiteboard. Don't limit yourself. You can rethink later. This exercise will give you a glimpse of what could be.

EXAMPLE - PARENTING APP

EXAMPLE - PARENT ADVOCATE

EXAMPLE - BIKE DESK

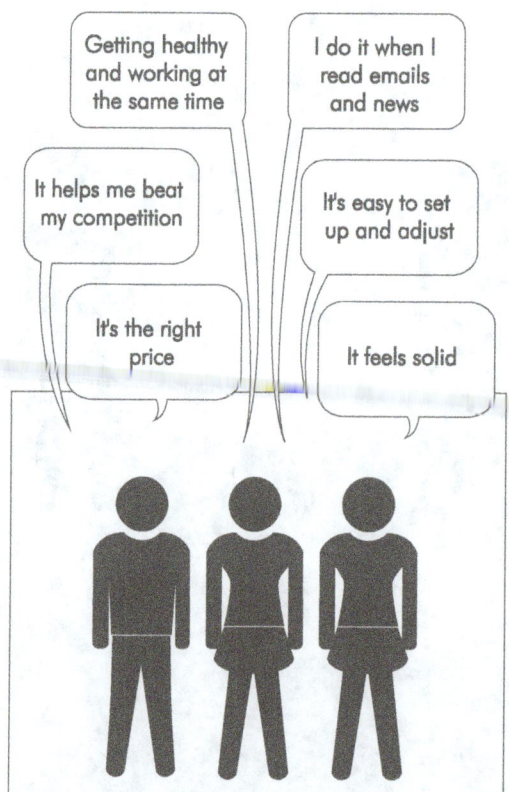

 ## Instructions

In a group or as an individual, draw out an idea sketch with the user or idea in the middle. Add all the possible stakeholders, constraints and assumptions. On the lower left hand corner, write out open questions in abbreviated form. On the lower right hand corner, scribble essential details in abbreviated form. Refine as needed.

1. Keep a journal of inspirational products and services.

2. Create a list of unmet needs that frustrate you.

3. Develop an "Imagine in 5 years…" sketch.

3. Set aside creative research time and creative practice time daily.

4. Observe patterns and ask "What if?" and follow with "If…then…"

5. Practice the idea sketch regularly.

FAQ

1. **What if I am not really creative?** Creativity is a mindset and a process. It is true that some people are more predisposed to creative endeavors. However, even the most creative people have a process so that they get work done on their uninspired days. It takes practice like everything else.

2. **Where do I find sources of inspiration?** It depends on what you want your enterprise to do. Besides the really practical Indiegogo and Kickstarter for products and services, medical journals and trade publications can be very useful. More general sources of inspiration include Pinterest, Etsy, and Instagram. Follow your passion on the web, journals, and magazines. Inspiration can come from anywhere.

Improvisation

To improvise is to compose, deliver or perform without preparation. You likely spend 80 percent of your waking time improvising. In almost every social interaction, and in nearly all meetings, you have improvised. You are most comfortable with the social interactions that you have practiced many times before, such as having dinner with family and friends, or a department meeting.

Infrequent social interactions or meetings are often the most awkward or exhilarating. Mastering these events is often where you develop the most. The need to connect the dots quickly during these events leads to considerable creative growth.

Improvisation happens best in groups. Charles Darwin wrote, "in the long history of humankind (and animal kind, too) those who learned to collaborate and improvise most effectively have prevailed." Group improvisation usually leads to faster recognition of a changed reality and effective outcomes.

Naturally, groups often do best with good chemistry of members who have different skillsets and perspectives. The challenge is that good chemistry can be difficult with members who have different perspectives. The key is to establish trust by creating authentic relationships and through personal storytelling. Good chemistry will get a team through setbacks and personal differences.

A basketball coach will say that a team with great chemistry often beats a more talented team with lesser chemistry. In business, teams are often assigned to projects that require difficult tradeoffs with only a perfunctory attempt to establish rapport.

Considerable effort should be invested in developing authentic relationships. If the team knows each member's personal story, then it is easier to be empathetic and understand the context of the member's contribution and personal biases. With this foundation, it is easier to create a "no fail" environment where members feel confident that their ideas will not be mocked.

Good Chemistry = Authentic Relationships + Empathy + Respect + Validation + Different Skills

Good Chemistry ≠ Always Agree

Great Team = Creative Conflict + Respect

Validation is important for building rapport. Freely give praise for genuinely good ideas. Be authentic about expressing your likes.

Good chemistry doesn't mean that everybody is always in agreement. In fact, having different viewpoints and backgrounds will likely facilitate creative conflict. The key feature is having respect for others by letting them express and consider their ideas even if you don't agree. Trying to win every battle may be good for the ego, but is usually a setback for finding optimal solutions.

The goal is to create a playful environment, where members can take chances by offering divergent ideas. In comedy improvisation, there is the term "crazytown," where the scene goes to the absurd. However, the best creative ideas are often found on just outside of "crazytown." A team member may propose a crazy idea where everyone laughs along. Then another member suggests a similar idea that is more plausible. This area is often where the best ideas are found.

While group improvisation may feel messy, divergent thinking is enhanced and multiplied in an unstructured environment.

In comedy improvisation, warm up exercises are always used to create the playful environment to encourage creativity and authentic relationships. A number of these exercises have been included below. The creation of a playful environment generally leads to dramatically improved outcomes – and a lot more fun.

Ideation Rules

1. Create a no fail zone. Don't make judgments on any ideas. The key is to make sure all group members have the trust of other members so that they can say anything. At times, a group member may suggest an outlandish idea which leads another member to think up a great idea. Develop a "no fail" group mentality.

2. Create lots of ideas. The goal of ideation is to come up with as many ideas as possible. Edit later.

3. Create a "Yes and..." mindset. When another group member says an idea, say "yes and" add more to the idea. Never use a "no but" in ideation. Be aware of your facial expressions and posture.

4. Listen, don't think. Have fun. Listen to other group members and react. Don't let your pre-existing thoughts slow the energy. Go with it. If you have fun, everyone will have fun.

5. Make your teammates look and feel great. Try to add as much as you can to what your teammates offer. Give them validation by actively telling them what you like about their comments.

6. Don't steamroll. Present your idea. If it does not get traction, let it go. Don't lock into your idea and stop listening to others.

Editing Rules

1. My take is. Start your suggestion with "My take, my view, from my perspective" or some variant. There qualifications suggest humility, which is easier for the idea generator to accept.

2. Start with the positive. It is easier to take criticism when it's delivered with a positive attitude. Tell the idea originator what you like and make constructive criticism along with offering a potential solution. Be specific in your suggestions. Don't use "it doesn't work for me." Instead try "It may work better if." This approach will take practice.

3. Don't try to win every battle. There is an adage, "If you win every argument in a marriage, you won't be married for long." This applies to the group. No one likes someone who thinks they are right all the time, even if they are. Let it go.

4. Remember "It's about the idea, not you." Do your best to detach your emotions from the idea. If it is your idea, let go of the ego and listen objectively. Better to hear the comments now than when you have already spent time and money on the idea. If you are making the suggestion, be as delicate and positive as you can. The mindset is idea first, team second and you third.

FAQ & Resources

What if I am not much of a team player?

Collaboration is key to starting a successful business. Skills are developed after much practice. You will need other people's help to scale the business. Other people's perspectives will be critical to honing your business.

What if my idea does not get chosen?

Let it go. Save the idea and work on it yourself later.

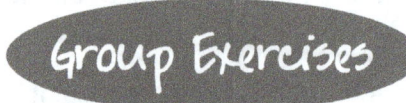

Group exercises are a great way to develop innovative ideas. Different perspectives and positive energy are essential to creativity. The goal is to get participants to an almost child-like, playful state of mind. At times, the atmosphere will be silly, crazy and fun. There are no wrong answers. The more ideas, the better.

Many of these exercises are used in comedy improvisation, while others are modified specifically for innovation and entrepreneurship. The exercises usually last for 3-5 minutes or when a natural break point occurs, whichever comes first.

Warm Up Exercises

Zip Zap Zop

The purpose of this exercise is to get all group members focused on each other by listening and making eye contact. All group members stand in a circle. The first member points to a second member and says "zip." The second member points to a third member and says "zap." The third member points to a fourth member and says "zop." The fourth member points to another member and says "zip," starting the whole word game over. The key is to keep up a fast pace. There are no mistakes, just keep going if the words are out of order. Once the members get better, change the word pattern to "zip zip zap zap zop zop zop."

Clapping Hands

The purpose of this exercise is to get all group members focused on each other by listening, making eye contact and mirroring. All group members stand in a circle. The first member turns to a member beside them and claps. The second member makes eye contact and claps at the same time. The second member turns to a third member and they both clap at the same time. The clapping should go around the circle twice. Once members get better, clap twice. Finally, allow members to change direction.

One Word Story

The purpose of this exercise is to get all group members focused as a team by telling a collective story. All group members stand in a circle. The first member says one word, usually a noun. Going clockwise in the circle, the second member says a word, usually a verb. The third member says a word to further the sentence. The story continues to grow, usually for 2-3 times around the circle, until there is a conclusion.

Mirror & Heighten

The purpose of this exercise is to learn how to mirror your partner's emotion and heighten it. In business, this is an essential skill for building rapport. There are four core emotions: happy, sad, mad and scared. After getting a suggestion of a location or occupation, the first player starts the scene with an understated emotion like happy. The second player reads and expresses the emotion a little more in physical appearance and how they speak. The first player reads and expresses the emotion even more to heighten the state. This dialog goes until the extreme in the emotion is reached. In the advanced game, one of the players begins to lower the emotion gradually so the dialog gets back to the original emotional level.

Word Association

The purpose of this exercise is to get all group members to work as a group. All group members stand in a circle. The first player starts with a word, say "squirrel." A second player next to the first says an associated word like "nut." A third player says an associated word like "tree." The game goes around the circle twice. In and advanced version, the group tries to word associate back to the original word.

Instant Expert: Clark Kent/Superman

The purpose of this exercise is to practice self-awareness and different personas. One group member stands in the middle of a circle formed by the rest of the group. A subject is suggested and as well as the persona of either Superman or Clark Kent. The member in the middle pretends he is an expert on the subject, often by making things up. Her/his persona should be confident and strong if the suggested persona is Superman, or meek and scholarly if the persona is Clark Kent. After 30 seconds, someone is the group says the opposite persona and the person in the middle must switch. The key is to learn how to take on different personas while talking about things you don't know about.

Turning Point

The purpose of this exercise is to help group members establish authentic relationships quickly. Group members stand in a semi circle. Standing in the middle of the semi circle, the first member talks about 2-3 decisions that significantly affected their lives. Each member has 4-5 minutes to speak and the group can ask questions for 2-3 minutes. The key is that all members are candid and respectful of other members. It's best to do this exercise after 1-2 other warm up exercises and follow up with another warm up exercise.

Advanced Exercises

Where is My Celery?

The purpose of this exercise is to increase teamwork. The suggestion should be a category like cars, colors, or fruits. All group members stand in a circle. Use cars as an example. The first member points to another member and says an example of a car like "Ford." The second member points to another member and says "Toyota." This happens until everyone in the group has had a turn. The group repeats the loop 2-3 times. In the advanced game, the group simultaneously plays with two categories. The group starts a first category and then creates a second category. Finally, they combine the two by starting with the first category and then adding the second category a minute later. This mindbender of two categories is great for becoming aware of all the members of the team.

New Choice

The purpose of this exercise is to promote divergent thinking. Two group members stand in the middle of a circle formed by the rest of the group. Any word suggestion is made to the duo. After 2-3 lines are exchanged, a group leader says NEW CHOICE. The member who said the last line creates a new line and scene then carries on. After 2-3 more lines, the group leader says NEW CHOICE. The member who said the last line creates a new line and then carries on. The group leader should end the scene at a logical point, typically after 2-3 minutes.

Six Through the Door

The purpose of this exercise is to promote divergent thinking. One group member stands in the middle of a circle formed by the rest of the group. A suggestion is made to the member in the middle. The member in the middle's objective is to create six characters in 60 seconds, usually with one line to create a character. The member can use different accents, postures and lines to create 6 diverse characters. This exercise pace is usually frantic and lots of fun. The key is not to think too much.

Applied Exercises

Try That on for Size

The purpose of this exercise is for group members to share cool ideas and stimulate new ones. All group members stand in a circle. The group has prepared for this exercise by looking at Kickstarter, Indigogo, Fast Company, Wired and other cool product/service blogs. The first player shares the cool idea, product or service and then finishes by saying "Try that on for size!" The second player can build on the cool idea and finishes by saying "Try that on for size!" When the momentum slows, another member can share another cool idea and says "Try that on for size!" and the pattern repeats.

What I Find so Frustrating...

The purpose of this exercise is for group members to begin to ideate in a group setting. All group members stand in a circle. One member says "what I find so frustrating is..." and finishes the statement. All the members say "yeah!" and cheer the statement. A second member repeats what the first member said and adds the statement. All the members say "yeah!" and cheer the statement. A third member repeats what the second member said and adds the statement. This goes on until the idea has gone as far as it can. Then, another member begins again with "what I find so frustrating is..." and finishes the statement. The pattern continues.

Yeah, We can Fix That...

The purpose of this exercise is for group members to ideate in a group setting. All group members stand in a circle. On member repeats a "what I find so frustrating is..." statement from the previous exercise. A second player says "Yeah, we can fix that.." and finishes the statement. All the members say yeah and cheer the statement. A third player says "Yeah, we can fix that.." and finishes the statement by adding on to what the second member said or going in a different direction. All the members say yeah and cheer the statement. When the group runs out of ideas, then another member can begin the pattern again with "what I find so frustrating is..." statement from the previous exercise..

Yeah, That Rocks!

The purpose of this exercise is for members to solicit additional suggestions for their ideas from the group. All group members stand in a circle. The first member explains their idea in no more than one minute and ends it by saying "Yeah, that rocks!" All the members say "yeah!" and cheer. A second member makes a "Yes and..." suggestion and finishes with a "Yeah, that rocks!" All the members say "yeah!" and cheer. This pattern goes on until momentum slows, then another player starts a new exercise by explaining their idea.

These exercises will help you get to a playful, open state of mind. Silly, over-the-top is good. Often, one step inside silly is where the most creative ideas come from. Practice these exercises regularly with group members and trust levels will rise. The enhanced trust will allow members to push the boundaries of creativity, often with productive and hilarious results.

Design Thinking

OVERVIEW

Design Thinking is a problem-solving process of channeling creativity into finding problems and creating solutions. The method is based on repeated improvements based on research, frequent customer feedback and ideation from a diverse design team. Design Thinking is not rocket surgery; it is a straightforward problem-solving technique not too different from the scientific method.

The goal is clear: Create a solution - detailed product or service specifications - that has been vetted through repeated interactions with all stakeholders. These include the different user types, suppliers and providers.

Design Thinking has been described in many different ways from 3 steps to 17 steps. The names and number of steps can be different but the ritual is the same. We have developed the PRICE method, mostly because it is easier to remember. Here is a brief introduction:

To understand the innovation process, take note of the acronym PRICE, which refers to Problem and user Identification, Research, Improvise, Curating, and Editing. Let us take a look at the five steps (PRICE) in the innovation process.

1. Problem identification: Clearly lay out the problem and the key frustrations related to it. Finish the phrase "I don't like that..." Get as much feedback as you can from potential users. Learn more about their environment and perceptions to help you understand the problem and so you can formulate an appropriate solution. In the end, it's all about the users and how your solution addresses their concerns.

2. Research: Conduct research on the problem, the available solutions, and the solution providers. Understand the landscape clearly. Google solution providers and talk to customers. Pretend that you are a detective looking for all possible options. Skipping this process may lead to a duplication of a concept, a product, or a service that already exists. With proper research, on the other hand, you can avoid wasting time and effort. With enough accurate information, you can focus on finding gaps and understanding current inadequacies in current solutions, if there are any, and then start developing a better solution.

3. Improvisation: Think of as many potential solutions as you can. Be messy. Overshoot on the ideas. Write them down no matter how crazy they may seem. Don't be critical in this stage; just come up with a ton of ideas. When you get stuck, ask "what if?" to keep going.

4. Curating: Study the potential solutions side by side, and consider ways to combine them. Leave all options on the table, and remix the ideas. Then start classifying and identifying the best concepts.

5. Editing: Eliminate ideas based on benefits, costs, and feasibility. Distill your options down to the most realistic solution with the highest value.

The PRICE process can feel cumbersome and awkward. You might be tempted to edit before you are done with the ideation and curating steps. Keep in my mind, though, that innovation takes time. It does not follow a straight line; it zigs and zags. Be patient and keep practicing. Often, the process involves building layers on top of each other.

Problem

Assume a discovery mindset, namely that the final product/service will be different from what you currently think it to be. The process starts with a premise, validates with other stakeholders, especially users, as many times as needed to create clear product/service specifications.

An individual or group defines what type of problem they want to solve. In some cases, a designer has a general notion in mind. For example, they want to reduce the achievement gap in public schools or create a biometric device for athletes. In other cases, a designer has a more specific goal in mind: create a parent advocate for low-wealth families or design a running gait analysis tool using sensors on clothing.

Here are some common pitfalls. Most often, product designers have a technology or capability in search of a market. It is natural to conclude what is the easiest path to market based on extending the technology. In addition, entrepreneurs will see a need that they have, check with friends who have a favorable review and start a business. In both cases, initial bias clouds the judgment of users' wants. Technology and an entrepreneur's passion are important, but both are secondary considerations to the user's wants and willingness to pay for a solution.

PITFALLS
1. Technology chases easiest market
2. Ask friends during validation
   - check users wants and willingness to pay early

The problem definition starts with identifying the user and their pain point. An ideal mindset would be one of problem detection, which requires gathering information and then drawing conclusions. In the beginning, no preconceptions should be fixed. The definition of user profiles and their pain points often change with new data.

IDENTIFY USER
1. ID User
2. Find pain point
   - Avoid Preconceptions
   - change with new data

In a perfect world, the problem, user and pain point definitions are done in a diverse group environment. Multiple perspectives more fully challenge assumptions. Ideally, each member would have spent quality time with the user to understand their story, mindset and preferences.

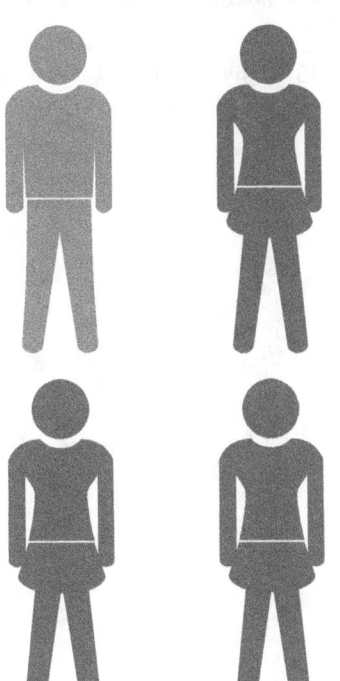

Essential Tools
1. User Profile
2. User Experience
3. Product/Service Haiku
   - Create diverse group

Customer Profile

Create a customer profile.

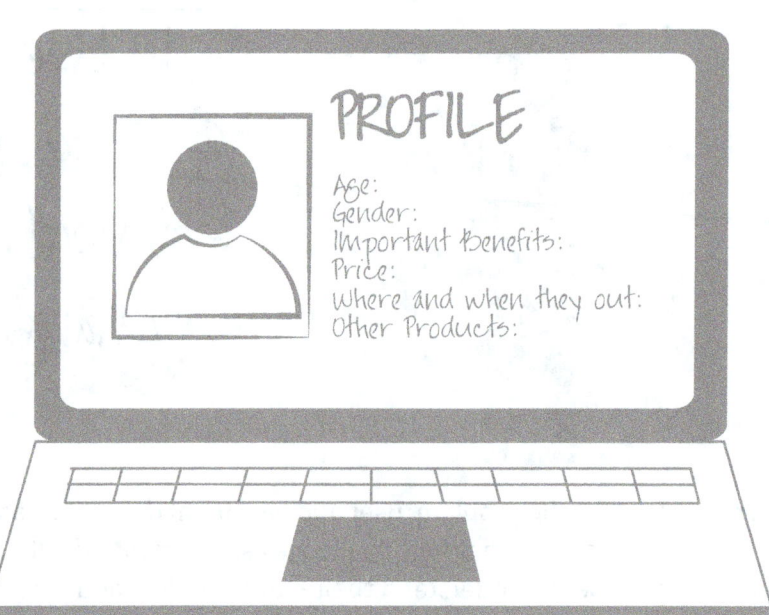

A customer profile in a business is like a main character description in a novel. The profile includes the necessary details to understand who the customer is.

A customer profile often includes the following information:

1. Age range
2. Gender
3. Most important benefits they care about
4. How important prices are to them
5. How they research a product
6. Where they buy
7. When they buy
8. Whether they do repeat buys
9. Adjacent products they buy (e.g., toothbrush and toothpaste)
10. Which competitor product they use

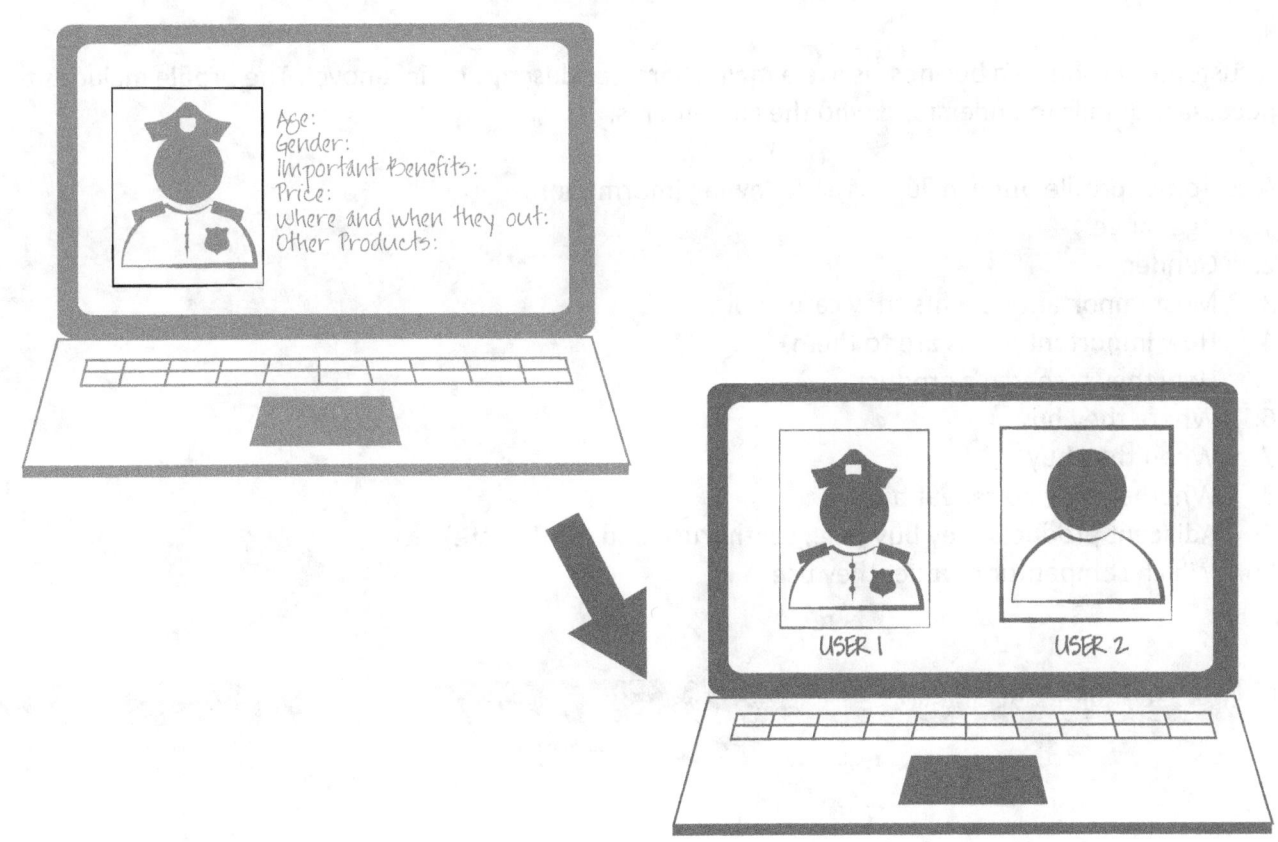

Let's look at an example: Deidre noticed that female police officers often complained about how uncomfortable wearing bulletproof vests were. The cotton t-shirts sold in the uniform shops were too hot in warm weather and not warm enough in the winter. After talking to all the female police officers she knew, Deidre wrote out a customer profile.

The profile is as follows: females aged 28-45 years who want comfortable dark-colored undershirts in all-weather conditions. They want to pay $20–$35. While many look online, they only really buy products that they can try on. The officers said they would buy twice a year—a long-sleeved shirt in the fall and a short-sleeved shirt in the spring. They hope to get one year of use given that the vest constantly rubs the shirts. They would buy 10 shirts annually. Officers often buy undershirts when buying new uniforms.

Deidre made the following calculation: In the first year, the customer's annual purchase amount is 10 shirts at $30, or $300.

Two important things to consider:

1. Customer profiles can change. In Deidre's case, male police officers started asking about the product. Have a clear profile, but be open to changes.

2. There can be more than one customer profile in your business. In Deidre's case, she needed to sell to uniform store owners so that she could sell to the end customer, the police officers. She needs a customer profile for buyers at uniform stores.

A customer profile in a business is like a main character description in a novel. The profile includes the necessary details to understand who the customer is.

A customer profile often includes the following information:
1. Age range
2. Gender
3. Most important benefits they care about
4. How important prices are to them
5. How they research a product
6. Where they buy
7. When they buy
8. Whether they do repeat buys
9. Adjacent products they buy (e.g., toothbrush and toothpaste)
10. Which competitor product they use

CUSTOMER PROFILE - Create by filling out below.	Customer 1	Customer 2
Name		
Age range		
Gender		
Most important benefits they care about		
How important is price?		
How they research the product		
Where they buy		
When they buy (impulse, long research, seasonal)		
Is it a repeat buy? If so, what is the pattern?		
Adjacent products? (think toothbrush and toothpaste)		
Which competitor product do they use?		
Average Units Purchased Guesstimate		
Average Price Guesstimate		
Average Purchase Amount Guesstimate		
Average Marketing Investment Guesstimate		
Percentage Marketing / Purchasing (2-30%)		

EXAMPLE - BULLETPROOF ACTIVE WEAR

	Customer 1	Customer 2
Name	Low-wealth parents of children 0-6 yrs old	Uniform Store Owners
Age range	16-35	35-60
Gender	Female	Male
Most important benefits they care about	Respect; What is good for kids and community	Good margin
How important is price?	NA	Very important, won't spend more than $15-18
How they research the product	Word-of-mounth	Look online and at tradeshows
Where they buy	In neighborhood	Sales reps and tradeshows
When they buy (impulse, long research, seasonal)	After hearing from friends and attending sessions	Oct-Nov and May-June
Is it a repeat buy? If so, what is the pattern?	NA	Biannual with fill-ins
Adjacent products? (think toothbrush and toothpaste)	Preschool, babysitters, county services	Police uniforms
Which competitor product do they use?	NA	Sell mostly cotton T-shirts
Average Units Purchased Guesstimate	NA	200
Average Price Guesstimate	NA	$15
Average Purchase Amount Guesstimate	NA	3,000
Average Marketing Investment Guesstimate	NA	$100
Percentage Marketing / Purchasing (2-30%)	NA	3%

EXAMPLE - PLAYDATE APP

Linkedin meets match.com for kids playdates	Customer 1	Customer 2
Name	Parents of 3-14-year-old kids	Kids
Age range	30-55	3-14
Gender	Female mostly	Female Mostly
Most important benefits they care about	Background info on other kids and parents	Background info on other kids
How important is price?	$4.99-$9.99	No more than $9.99
How they research the product	Look online and word-of-mouth	Word of mouth
Where they buy	iTunes or Android	iTunes or Android
When they buy (impulse, long research, seasonal)	Impulse	Impulse
Is it a repeat buy? If so, what is the pattern?	No	No
Adjacent products? (think toothbrush and toothpaste)	LinkedIn	LinkedIn
Which competitor product do they use?	LinkedIn and Facebook	Facebook
Average Units Purchased Guesstimate	1	1
Average Price Guesstimate	$10	$10
Average Purchase Amount Guesstimate	$1	$1
Average Marketing Investment Guesstimate	$2	$2
Percentage Marketing / Purchasing (2-30%)	20%	20%

EXAMPLE - PARENT ADVOCATE

Education consultant for low-wealth parents	Customer 1	Customer 2
Name	Low-wealth parents of children 0-6 yrs old	School principals and social workers
Age range	16-35	22-60
Gender	Female	Female
Most important benefits they care about	Respect; What is good for kids and community	Easy to work with and reduce achievement gap
How important is price?	NA	NA
How they research the product	Word-of-mounth	Information sessions
Where they buy	In neighborhood	Information sessions
When they buy (impulse, long research, seasonal)	After hearing from friends and attending sessions	Information sessions
Is it a repeat buy? If so, what is the pattern?	NA	NA
Adjacent products? (think toothbrush and toothpaste)	Preschool, babysitters, county services	Other nonprofits
Which competitor product do they use?	NA	Other nonprofits
Average Units Purchased Guesstimate	NA	NA
Average Price Guesstimate	NA	NA
Average Purchase Amount Guesstimate	NA	NA
Average Marketing Investment Guesstimate	NA	NA
Percentage Marketing / Purchasing (2-30%)	NA	NA

EXAMPLE - BIKE DESK

	Customer 1	Customer 2
Name	White collar workers	Cycling enthusiasts
Age range	30-60	35-60
Gender	Male	Male
Most important benefits they care about	Get healthy	Get extra ride time
How important is price?	$300-$1,000	$600-$1,500
How they research the product	Look online but want to see before buying	Look online but want to see before buying
Where they buy	Office furniture store or online	Office furniture store or online
When they buy (impulse, long research, seasonal)	Long research mostly	Long research mostly
Is it a repeat buy? If so, what is the pattern?	No	No
Adjacent products? (think toothbrush and toothpaste)	Office furniture	Office furniture and bike shops
Which competitor product do they use?	LifeSpan	LifeSpan
Average Units Purchased Guesstimate	1	1
Average Price Guesstimate	$900	$1,200
Average Purchase Amount Guesstimate	$900	$1,200
Average Marketing Investment Guesstimate	$90	$120
Percentage Marketing / Purchasing (2-30%)	10%	10%

HOW

Develop a customer profile by filling out the profile template.

FAQ & Resources

1. What is an average transaction amount (ATA)?
This amount is the average value that a customer buys each time from a company.

2. What is the annual purchase amount (APA)?
This amount is the average value that a customer purchases each year.

Customer Experience

Share stories of your customer learning about and buying your product.

A. Customer experience refers to the interaction of a customer with a product or a service. You can share stories of customer experience where you describe how customers first learn about your product and its key benefits, their experience in purchasing it, their expectations, and their experience or perception of the product's performance, including any product issues. These stories reveal key company processes and needed marketing materials.

1. Specifically describe the customers and their needs.

2. Explain how the customers first learn about your product. How do they research the products (online, in-store, or product-by-product comparison)? Answers to these questions will determine what marketing materials or strategies you need to explore.

3. How does your product solve their problem? What is the key benefit? Responses to these should reflect your intended message to the customers.

4. How and where does the customer purchase the product? Data from these will show where the product should be sold.

5. What happens when the customer has a problem with the product? Information from this will help you develop processes to deal with product issues while maintaining a positive customer relationship. You will encounter product issues; being prepared is essential to converting an unhappy customer into a fiercely loyal customer.

CUSTOMER EXPERIENCE

1. Who is the customer?
2. How did they become aware of the product/service?
3. Where and how do they purchase/join the product/service?
4. What happens is there is a problem?

Note: Use a word document if you prefer.

EXAMPLE - PARENTING APP

Samantha is a 38 year old mother of two: Eli who is 3 years old and Alexi who is 6 years old. They live in an apartment and have some play dates but other kids and their families often have their own plans. In addition, Samantha's husband Steve does not click with the fathers of Eli's and Alexi's friends.

Samantha hears about the parent app from a college friend who lives in another city. Samantha had seen some Google Adwords when she did parenting searches but did not click on any. She goes on the App Store and reads the reviews. Though she has concerns about the number of local matches, she buys it anyway as it is only $4.99.

The App crashed often so she visited the app website and filed a complaint. Within 3 hours, she received a friendly email with a checklist of potential solutions and a telephone number to call if those did not work. She realized her iOS needed to be updated and afterwards, the app worked fine. She was ready to start using the app.

EXAMPLE - BIKE DESK

Christian is a 43-year-old graphic designer who works from home. After his physician recommended that he lose weight, Christian started riding a bicycle. He really liked how some of his most creative ideas happened when he was riding.

Even though he'd seen Adwords for the Write Cycle Desk, Christian only became interested when he saw a short Bicycling magazine article about the desk. Christian bought the product online, especially because of the 100% money back guarantee including freight. He considered the desk-only option, but then thought an upright indoor bike/desk combination worked best for him. Christian reasoned that he would not be able able to do heavy graphic design on the Bike Desk, but he could read, answer emails and make Skype calls. The Write Bike Desk would not replace outdoor cycling but it would be a good way to build aerobic activity, particularly on rainy days.

Christian found the seat uncomfortable and had a question on how to adjust the handlebar height. He visited the website and watched videos on handlebar height adjustment. Christian called the company and left a voicemail. Within 4 hours, a customer service rep called back and offered several options for seats. Christian was pleased with his experience so far.

FAQ

What is the key benefit?
The key benefit is the one element that the customer most values in a product. For example, most customers value their iPhones because they organize their favorite music in one place. iPhones offer a variety of benefits, but for many customers, music organization is the key benefit.

Product Haiku

Develop a clear product/service definition by making specific tradeoffs.

A. Ideas are like nuggets that have to be hammered, treated, and shaped to become a product. Ideas are often fuzzy and huge, while a successful product/service is defined clearly by making tradeoffs.

B. A haiku is an ancient Japanese poem that is distilled down to the essence. Like a haiku, a clear product definition includes the problem you are trying to solve, who the user is, what the solution is, and its key features and benefits.

C. Once you have an idea, get the opinion of as many potential users as possible. The most common, and often disastrous, mistake is that entrepreneurs create products, services, and enterprises without getting input from the target users.

D. You should not assume that you know what the users want without actually checking with them first. Walk in their shoes. Understand their environment and what is important to them. Before finalizing a product or service definition, get the opinion of as many users as possible.

E. A product definition involves a set of tradeoffs made so that you have a clear idea of what your product is and is not. With this clear definition, you can test the concept with as many users and advisors as possible.

F. Understand the user universe as much as you can. Creating new products and services requires a great deal of study, revision, and refinement well before you actually start making or selling.

How

1. Develop a clear product/service definition by making specific tradeoffs.

2. Use the Product Haiku. Its structure will enable you to make the appropriate tradeoffs.

3. You will not likely know all the answers immediately. Research, think, and make decisions.

4. Complete the Haiku, keeping in mind that you can update it later with new information.

PRODUCT HAIKU		
Problem		
User	1	
	2	
	3	
Stakeholders	1	
	2	
	3	
Constraints	1	
	2	
	3	
	4	
	5	
Solution		
Key benefits	1	
	2	
	3	
Features	1	
	2	
	3	
	4	
	5	
How different?		
Price estimate?		
Develop cost?		
Next steps	1	
	2	
	3	
	4	
	5	

PRODUCT HAIKU	EXAMPLE - PARENTING APP	EXAMPLE - PARENTING ADVOCATE
Problem	Parents want to set up playdates with great kids and parents	Achievement gap established when kids are 0-6 years old
User	28-55 year old parents with 2-16 yr old kids	16-35 year old, low-wealth parents and their kids
	13-17 year old kids	Schools and school district
Stakeholders	1. Parents/Kids	1. Schools and school district
	2. Companies who sell kids/parenting products	2. State/county youth services
	3	3. Nonprofits
Constraints	Parents are time constrained; want ease of use	Current solution is Swiss cheese; gaps in key areas
	Parents spend much time with the parents of the kids' friends	Parents are suspicious of outside parties
	Hard to find good match of kids to kids and parents to parents	School district focused on K-12, not preschool
		Preschools don't have resources to deal outside the walls
Solution	A match.com/linkedin.com for kid's playdates	Parent Advocate promotes best practices in culturally sensitive way
Key benefits	1. Parents enjoy spending time with other great parents	1. Give parents access to best practices
	2. Kids are happy to play with likeable matches	2. Build community and awareness of local kids resources
	3. Find great kid-related businesses	3. Help school district better understand incoming students
Features	1. Easy-to-build profile builder	1. Parent meetings to learn about resources
	2. Easy search	2. In-house family visits
	3. Create communities	3. Local resource mapping guide
	4. Share parenting advice	4. Best practices curriculum for parents and kids
	5. Ratings on kid-related businesses	5. Organized playdates at schoosl and parks
How different?	No other competitors	Incomplete network in local communities
Price	$2.99-$9.99	NA
How to develop & cost?	Designer ($7K) Pilot app ($15K)	Curriculum Dev: $15K, Advocates $50K x 1 in Phase 1
Next steps	1. Hire graphic designer after developing design brief	1. Garner stakeholder support
	2. Select web developer	2. Develop curriculum
	3. Identify pilot area	3. Recruit advocates
	4. Develop marketing plan	4. Pilot program
	5	5

PRODUCT HAIKU	EXAMPLE - BIKE DESK
Problem	1. Want to excercise while working at desk
User	2. White collar workers
	3. Cycling enthusiasts
Stakeholders	1. Office equipment sellers and cycling bloggers
	2. Manufacturer
	3. Distribution
Constraints	1. Move and scale to market quickly
	2. Easy to assemble
	3. Small footprint
Solution	Desk with integrated bike
Key benefits	1. Great health and cycling benefits
	2. Peace of mind
	3.
Features	1. Solid feel to bike
	2. Smooth and quiet operating
	3. Easy to assemble
	4. Metric software
	5
How different?	Options at attractive price point
Price	$900
How to develop & cost?	$10K development
Next steps	1. Develop design brief and prototype
	2. Determine manufacturer
	3. Find distribution partner
	4. Create marekting collateral
	5

FAQ & Resources

What is the purpose of Haiku?

Haiku will help you transform a fuzzy idea into a specific definition. This process will require making hard decisions. Keep in mind that you can change them later, but you will always have a clear definition.

What if I don't know the answers?

In the beginning, you will not likely know all the answers. Research, think, and decide.

What do I do with Haiku?

This is the critical first step in developing a product or service. Test this product/service definition with your potential users. After several refinements you will be ready for prototyping.

Instructions

Goal: Develop an initial definition of the user and problem

Outcomes: First draft of User Profile, User Experience and Product/Service Haiku

Environment: Find an open space with a creative vibe if possible. Have access to blackboards, whiteboards or large tablets of paper, post-its, pens and timer.

Key Steps

1. Create playful atmosphere by warming up with group games found in the Improvise section.

2. Complete idea sketch on board or paper like that found in the Creative Mindset section.

3. Complete a user profile.

4. Write out a user experience.

5. Complete an "Imagine in 5 years…" sketch like that found in the Creative Mindset section.

6. Reconcile the idea sketch, user profile and customer experience so that they are consistent. Complete the Product Haiku.

7. Complete final run through of idea sketch, user profile, and customer experience with the team. Obtain sign-off from all team members.

In this section, we introduced the Problem, or the P in PRICE, the needed tools and the key steps.

Research

The research stage is absolutely essential but often undervalued. Designers and entrepreneurs often complete a light review because they already have a set idea. Unfortunately this may lead to designers developing ideas that already exist. It is hard to differentiate your product/service if you don't know the existing options. Don't be discouraged if you discover competitors until you complete research. The existence of competitors validates the opportunity.

The best place to start is online to develop some baseline fluency. The next step is spending time with experts including professors, consultants and vendors. An hour with them will likely save many hours of individual research. Complete a SWOT (Strengths, Weaknesses, Opportunities, and Threats) analysis and product features comparison on competitors. At this stage, complete at least 23 user-needs discovery surveys and distill the results into a user-needs analysis.

RESEARCH → FLUENCY

1. Online Search
2. Experts
3. Users
4. Stakeholders
5. SWOT
   - Share info on Cloud

The work is best divided between team members. The information is best shared online via cloud storage such as Google documents or Dropbox. In this way, all team members have access to research in real time and are fully prepared for the improvise stage.

Online Search

Conduct an online search of experts, comparable product/services, competitor websites, publications, books, patents and news. Type in the product/service and see where the search engine takes you. The template helps you divide the research into blocks. Share notes with others in the cloud.

ONLINE RESEARCH					
Product/Service Competitors		Relevant Experts			
Name	Website	Name			
Comment					
Name	Website	Relevant Associations			
		Title			
Comment					
		Relevant Research & Publications Title			
		Title	Website		
Name	Website				
Comment					
Name	Website				
Comment					

EXAMPLE - PARENTING APP

Product/Service Competitors		Relevant Experts			
Name	Website	Name	Title	Website	Email Phone
Match	www.match.com	Arthur Peters	Blogger	APeters.com	art@apeters.com
Great user interface, emulate their functionality, particularly search features		Sonny Williams	VP Social Networks	shing.com	SWilliams@shing.com
		Teresa Samuels	VP Social Networks	Vanage.com	Ts@vanage.com
Name	Website	Relevant Associations			
Linkedin	www.linkedin.com	Title	Contact	Website	
Strong profile information and easy serach. Really good "people also viewed" feature		Social Networks International	Vlad Holst	www.sni.com	
		Social Media Association	Michelle Purst	www.sma.com	
		Relevant Research & Publications Title			
		Title	Website		
Name	Website	Social Networks Quarterly	www.SNQ.com		
eHarmony	www.eHarmony.com	Fast Company	www.FastCompany.com		
Have some additional functionality and a slightly different search feature		Relevant Books			
		Title	Author		
		Social Networks Now	Keith Bonner		
		Niche Networks	Rose Richards		

EXAMPLE - PARENT ADVOCATE

Product/Service Competitors		Relevant Experts			
Name	Website	Name	Title	Website	Email/Phone
Harlem Children's Zone	http://hcz.org	Sandy Jones	Curriculum Manager	www.cdi.org	sjones@cdi.org
Great resource. They don't have much experience on 0-6 year olds. A real model for holistic solution. Great way to see pitfalls based on their expereinces. Their Baby College and Harlem Gems programs are most relevant.		Dawn Viceroy	Parent Advocate Mgr.	www.ccci.org	dviceroy@cci.org
		Geoff Reynolds	Professor	www.unc.edu	grey@unc.edu
Name	Website	Relevant Associations			
East Durham Children's Initative	http://edci.org	Title	Website		
Strong profile information and easy serach. Really good "people also viewed" feature		Childcare Exchange	http://www.childcareexchange.com		
		Early Childhood News	www.earlychildhoodnews.com/		
		Relevant Research & Publications Title			
		Childcare Exchange	Website		
Name	Website	Early Childhood News	www.SNQ.com		
eHarmony	www.eHarmony.com	SECA	www.FastCompany.com		
Have some additional functionality and a slightly different search feature		Relevant Books			
		Title	Author		
		Waiting for Superman	Geoffrey Canada		

EXAMPLE - BIKE DESK

Product/Service Competitors		Relevant Experts			
Name	Website	Name	Title	Website	Email Phone
LifeSpan Fitness	http://www.lifespanfitness.com	Jessica Tandy	Research Director	www.foe.org	jtandy@foe.org
First mover with good looking product. Category leader. Higher price point and untested cycling unit.		Ted Norris	Analyst	oef.org	norris@oef.org
		Tonya Cole	Asst. Professor	www.xavier.edu	tcole@xavier.edu
Name	Website	Relevant Associations			
Desk Cycle	http://deskcycle.com	Title	Contact	Website	
Very inexpensive under existing desk unit.		Fitness Office Equipment Assn	Paul Reaks	www.foea.org	
		Relevant Research & Publications Title			
		Title	Website		
Name	Website	Fitness Office Equip Newsletter	www.FOENewsletter.com		
Sunny Desk Cycle	http://sunnydeskcycle.com	Fast Company			
Really cheap pedaling-only units.		Relevant Books			
		Title	Author		

 Features Comparison

A side-by-side comparison of the proposed product/service versus existing ones creates clarity on the differences. Most competitor features are available online.

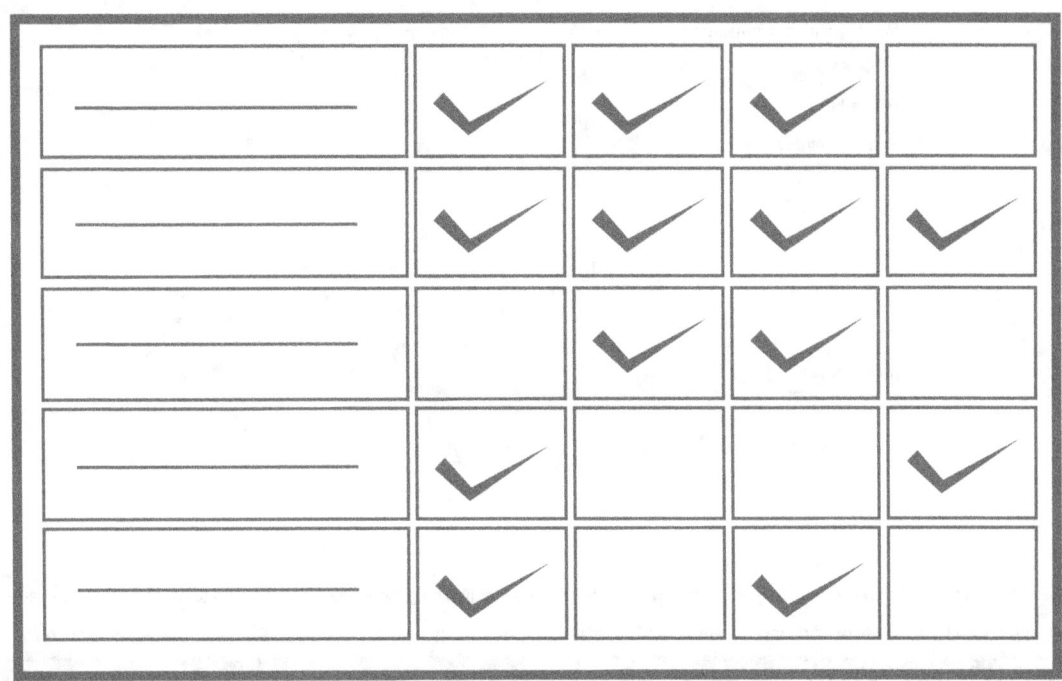

50

FEATURES COMPARISON

Company:				
Key Benefit				
Price				
Features				
Advantages				
Shortcomings				

EXAMPLE - PARENTING APP

Company:	Parenting App			
Key Benefit	Learn about other parents			
	Learn about other kids' likes			
	Build community			
	Meet new friends outside circle			
Price	$2.99-$9.99			
	Profile builder			
	Search features			
	Create groups			
Features				
Advantages	Niche focused			
Shortcomings	Needs to scale			

Notes: There are great social networks but there is not one with the specific goal of finding good matches for parents to other like-minded parents and kids with other like-minded kids. Facebook and Linkedin are best of breed and we can identify best functions from their sites and apply to our own.

EXAMPLE - PARENTING ADVOCATE

Company:	Parenting Advocate	Harlem Childrens Zone	EDCI	
Key Benefit	Reduce achievement gap	Reduce achievement gap	Reduce achievement gap	
	Parent support	Parent support	Parent support	
	Kids get equal opportunity	Kids get equal opportunity	Kids get equal opportunity	
	Build community	Build community	Build community	
Price	NA	NA	NA	
Features	Parent cheerleader	Parent cheerleader	Parent cheerleader	
	Parenting classes	Parenting classes	Parenting classes	
	In-home visits	In-home visits	In-home visits	
	Partner with school	Truly holistic support	Almost holistic support	
		Graduate to next program	Graduate to next program	
		Fully integrated with school	Partner with school	
Advantages	Smaller target group	Well funded	Well funded	
Shortcomings	Phased approach	Big urban challenges	Urban challenges	
	Less funding			

Notes: Our program can learn from the experiences and offerings of HCZ and EDCI. Our target audience is much smaller and the community has comparatively more resources though the program does not.

EXAMPLE - BIKE DESK

Company:	LifeSpan Fitness	DeskCycle	Sunny Desk Cycle	
Key Benefit	Excercise while you work	Excercise while you work	Excercise while you work	
Price	$1,100	$160	$49	
Features	Adjustable desk	Quiet magnetic resistance	Dial in resistance	
	Matching bike unit	Low height	Portable unit	
	Tracking software	5 function display		
	Small footprint			
Advantages	Modular system	Compact unit	Cheap	
	Good distribution	Easy to store	Small unit	
Shortcomings	High price	Not real cycling unit	Not real cycling unit	
	Insufficient cycle for enthusiasts		Questionable quality	

Notes: The gaps are a well-made product that has a solid cycling unit at a middle price point. Software would be a nice add-on feature. The low end of the market is saturated.

Expert Interviews

Experts interviews are a way to fast-track discovery and provide focus. Experts include professors and consultants. A one-hour meeting with an expert will likely save you hours of individual research time and open new possibilities. While staying on track is important, open-ended questions can lead to unexpected directions. As you would expect, face-to-face meetings are usually more helpful than telephone calls. Most will experts will give you an hour of their time. Ask for referrals to find additional experts.

EXPERT

- Very efficient
- Open new possibilities
- Repeat as needed

The best time to have the first expert interviews is after doing online research for initial discovery. In addition, expert meetings are helpful once you have completed a features comparison and SWOT analysis. Finally, another round of interviews is helpful after you complete the user interviews and analysis. Most likely, you will not be able to find an expert willing to do three meetings with you without compensation. Having different experts during the discovery process has its advantages.

EXPERT INTERVIEWS
EXPERT:
What is your opinion of the product/service?
What key benefits are users seeking?
What is the primary market for this product/service?
What is the secondary market for this product/service?
What assumptions and constraints do you see in the user base?
Who are the key stakeholders and what are their needs?
When and why do individuals use this kind of product/service?
Explain a typical session using the product
What do users enjoy about current products?
What do users not like about current products?
What are the key issues before users select?
What improvements do you suggest?

EXAMPLE - PARENTING APP

SALLY STEVENS, PARENTING BLOGGER

What is your opinion of the product/service?

I see a need for finding good matches for playdates. It does feel a little odd to use an app, but linkedin.com must have been weird at first. Parents may be put off about providing education and employment but they secretly want to know these details about other parents.

What key benefits are users seeking?

Parents want great playmates for their kids and want to spend time with parents with similar values.

What is the primary market for this product/service?

Urban, higher income families.

What is the secondary market for this product/service?

Aspirational income families.

What assumptions and constraints do you see in the user base?

Finding playmates via an app seems off-putting. How do you validate info?

Who are the key stakeholders and what are their needs?

Companies selling product to kids/tweens and teenagers. They want a return on building awareness.

When and why do individuals use this kind of product/service?

When child is 2-7 years old or moving to new neighborhood.

Explain a typical session using the product

I imagine that it is the same as linkedin.com or match.com.

What do users enjoy about current products?

Word of mouth is trustworthy.

What do users not like about current products?

Word of mouth is trustworthy but not scalable. Can't extend beyond current circle of friends.

What are the key issues before users select?

Is the information trustworthy and will I have sufficient privacy?

What improvements do you suggest?

Clear security measures. Validation of parent info possibly through partnership with Linkedin.

EXAMPLE - PARENT ADVOCATE

PAUL BIVENS, FAMILY SPECIALISTS ADVOCACY

What is your opinion of the product/service?

I like the concept of having parent advocates that provide parenting best practices for low-wealth parents with kids aged 0-6.

It will be very hard to walk the fine line of providing help and respecting the culture. Community and school buy-in will be key.

Realize other issues will arise.

What key benefits are users seeking?

Parents want what is best for their kids as they define best. Knowledge of what services are available is helpful.

What is the primary market for this product/service?

Low-wealth parents with kids aged 0-6 in six targeted neighborhoods.

What is the secondary market for this product/service?

NA

What assumptions and constraints do you see in the user base?

Users are suspicious of outsiders and the school district. Funding for essential services is scarce.

Who are the key stakeholders and what are their needs?

School district, county services, nonprofits. Each has its own mission and metrics.

When and why do individuals use this kind of product/service?

Parents are hungry for information and seek info when children are 0-3.

Explain a typical session using the product

Parents have access to some resources but are not aware of others. Home visits are infrequent with little follow-up due to insufficient resournces. Services outside the neighborhood are rarely used.

What do users enjoy about current products?

It often comes down to the personal touch.

What do users not like about current products?

Parents are resentful about the hodgepodge of service offerings.

What are the key issues before users select?

Personal relationships must be built over time.

What improvements do you suggest?

Community buy-in and real connector needed for parent advocate position.

EXAMPLE - BIKE DESK
JESSICA TANDY, FITNESS OFFICE EQUIPMENT ASSOCIATION

What is your opinion of the product/service?

Sensible entry given that there is high and low price point. Overall category is continuing to grow 20%+ annually. Appealing to office workers and cycling enthusiasts may be tough. May need to focus on one segment first.

What key benefits are users seeking?

Improve health while working.

What is the primary market for this product/service?

Independent workers 30-60 years old.

What is the secondary market for this product/service?

Cycling enthusiasts wanting to get more ride time in.

What assumptions and constraints do you see in the user base?

Easy to set up and small footprint.

Who are the key stakeholders and what are their needs?

Distribution is key while Minimum Order Quantities will be big issue with manufacturers.

When and why do individuals use this kind of product/service?

Want exercise while working.

Explain a typical session using the product

Users ride bike when they check email, read news and watch videos.

What do users enjoy about current products?

One stop purchase. Nice electrical height desk.

What do users not like about current products?

Price point given the quality of the cycling unit.

What are the key issues before users select?

Price and how solid the unit feels.

What improvements do you suggest?

Higher performing cycling unit.

Stakeholder Interviews

Like expert interviews, stakeholder interviews are a great way to discover reality quickly. Stakeholders include possible suppliers, partners, accreditation organizations, related agencies and enterprises in the area. It is important to get their view on the existing products/services and understand their constraints and needs. If applicable, get their view on the user and the market/area. These interviews will likely provide more details on how you can serve your user.

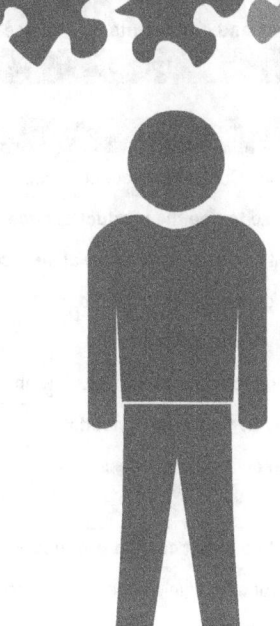

STAKEHOLDER
- Understand needs of suppliers, partners, agencies, etc.

STAKEHOLDER INTERVIEWS

Manufacturer

How would you like to see the product/service improve?

What are your key constraints?

What are your key organization's needs?

What do you not like about current products?

What improvements do you suggest?

What are the key benefits that the user is seeking?

What is the primary market for this product/service?

What is the secondary market for this product/service?

What assumptions and constraints do you see in the user base?

EXAMPLE - PARENTING APP

VP Marketing of Kids Consumer Products Company

How would you like to see the product/service improve?

I like the idea but it comes down to scale at the local level to prosper and scale at the national level for use to get interested.

What are your key constraints?

We back marketing projects that are proven winners.

What are your key organization's needs?

We are focused on buidling awareness but call-to-action programs are even more interesting.

What do you not like about current products?

We are always looking for highly targeted audience platforms.

What improvements do you suggest?

A database which is searchable so we can run highly targeted campaigns.
If applicable...

What are the key benefits that the user is seeking?

Parents ideally would like to spend time with other cool parents assuming their kids get along.

What is the primary market for this product/service?

Urban, high income, tech saavy parents

What is the secondary market for this product/service?

NA

What assumptions & constraints do you see in the user base?

STAKEHOLDER INTERVIEWS

EXAMPLE - PARENT ADVOCATE

School District Administrator

How would you like to see the product/service improve?

I really like the concept of reducing the achievement gap before they join the district.

What are your key constraints?

Time and money.

What are your key organization's needs?

We can participate but only if it is easy for us to participate.

What do you not like about current products?

The achievement gap has not changed in our district for 25 years. We need to try something different.

What improvements do you suggest?

We would like to see more evidence-based programs. I realize it is early days but we are a conservative organization.

If applicable...

What are the key benefits that the user is seeking?

Equal learning opportunities for their kids relative to others.

What is the primary market for this product/service?

Low-wealth parents with aged 0-6 year old kids in the selected neighborhoods.

What is the secondary market for this product/service?

NA

What assumptions and constraints do you see in the user base?

Users have low trust levels for outsiders. It will take time to build relationships.

EXAMPLE - BIKE DESK

Manufacturer

How would you like to see the product/service improve?

Cycling unit can be made to feel solid.

What are your key constraints?

Lead time of 20 weeks and minimum order quantities of 10,000 units.

What are your key organization's needs?

Firm order and sales forecast.

What do you not like about current products?

NA

What improvements do you suggest?

Heavier guage tubing and belt drive for easier maintence

If applicable...

What are the key benefits that the user is seeking?

NA

What is the primary market for this product/service?

NA

What is the secondary market for this product/service?

NA

What assumptions and constraints do you see in the user base?

NA

User Interviews

The User interviews are likely the most important step in defining your enterprise. While everyone agrees on this point, few people actually do a sufficient number. The right number is to complete at least 23 face-to-face interviews when testing ideas and prototypes. An online target is at least 230 surveys.

Be intentional on defining the users who should reflect your user profile. Choose users whom you don't know. Position yourself as ther person doing research on the product/service rather than as the inventor in order to get more objective feedback. Don't be burdened by preconceived notions.

The goal is to gather data, not to convince the user what they do or do not want. Ask the user to demonstrate how they use the product/service. Use a prototype when possible as visual learners represent two-thirds of the population. Inquire about their likes, dislikes and how they would improve the prototype. Ask them to help prioritize their needs. While having the questions serve as guide posts, let the interview take its own direction.

Goal: Gather data, not convince

Who:
- Clearly define user
- Users you don't know
- 23 face-to-face, 230 online

How:
- Ask users to describe or how they use the product
- Understand likes / dislikes and priorities
- Let interview take its direction
- Be open to latent, unspoken needs

Be open to latent needs, or those needs that the user may not even be aware of. Pay particular attention to nonverbal communication. They may state one preference, but their actions may indicate another.

USER INTERVIEWS

When and why do you use this kind of product/service?	
Explain how you use the product	
What do you enjoy about current products?	
What do you dislike about current products?	
What are the key issues when buying?	
What improvements do you suggest?	
What are the most important points we should understand?	
Remember:	Note:
Position yourself as researcher rather than owner.	
Clearly define the user.	
Let go of preconceived notions.	
Determine user priorities.	
Be aware of latent needs.	

When and why do you use this kind of product/service?	I want to find playmates for my son and daughter. It would be nice if I could find kids with parents whom I enjoy.
Explain how you use the product	Go on iPhone Apps and buy. I would create a profile page and then do a search for possible playdates in the area.
What do you enjoy about current products?	Word of mouth and random meetings at playgrounds is how it happens now.
What do you dislike about current products?	Don't really know who the parents are and the kids' interests.
What are the key issues when buying?	Privacy is an important issue and are there enough other users.
What improvements do you suggest?	Sounds good for now.
What is the most important points we should understand?	I'm willing to try it for $3.99.
Remember:	
Position yourself as researcher rather than owner.	
Clearly define the user.	
Let go of preconceived notions.	
Determine user priorities.	
Be aware of latent needs.	

EXAMPLE PARENTING ADVOCATE

When and why do you use this kind of product/service?	When my children are young. I feel ike I am missing out on something.
Explain how you use the product	I would attend the information sessions. If I like them, then I would sign up for the free classes.
What do you enjoy about current products?	Really nothing out there now. Just people I know in neighborhood.
What do you dislike about current products?	Feel kind of alone; I feel I may be missing something.
What are the key issues when buying?	I don't want people talking down to me. I need to know the person.
What improvements do you suggest?	Sounds good but has to be in the neighborhood.
What is the most important points we should understand?	Has to be with someone I know and trust.
Remember:	
Position yourself as researcher rather than owner.	
Clearly define the user.	
Let go of preconceived notions.	
Determine user priorities.	
Be aware of latent needs.	

EXAMPLE BIKE DESK

When and why do you use this kind of product/service?	I use when I am checking emails, reading online, or watching video. This is like free exercise while I work.
Explain how you use the product	I get on bike in the morning and after lunch.
What do you enjoy about current products?	The current unit is just ok. The desk is good quality with the electric adjustment.
What do you dislike about current products?	The seat is super wide and it does not feel like a real bike.
What are the key issues when buying?	The quality and how solid the unit feels.
What improvements do you suggest?	A real cycling unit with a real seat.
What is the most important points we should understand?	Needs to feel solid. Want good customer service. Need a good return policy to give me confidence.
Remember:	Note: A solid, real cycling unit seem to be the key takeaways.
Position yourself as researcher rather than owner.	
Clearly define the user.	
Let go of preconceived notions.	
Determine user priorities.	
Be aware of latent needs.	

User Analysis

Let's analyze the interview content. The goal is to translate customer needs into product/service features. First, interpret the stated customer needs using the following criteria:

1. Categorize the needs in product uses, likes, dislikes and suggestions

2. Be as specific as possible using affirmative statements, not negative.

3. State what the product can do, not how it will do it or what the product user can do.

4. Include the users' priority when possible.

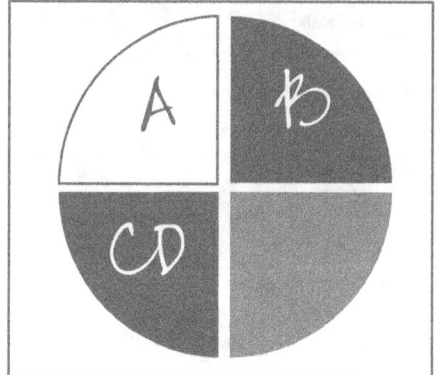

Goal: Translate needs into features

Prepare:
1. Categorize uses, likes/dislikes, suggestions
2. Be specific
3. State what product can do

How:
1. Group similar needs
2. Name groups
3. Develop prioritized needs list
4. Consider follow up survey

Once you have translated the user needs into a shared phraseology, the team can group the needs.

1. Place similar needs into groups by using cards, stickies, or spreadsheets.

2. After eliminating repeated or identical needs, name the group based on similarity of the needs.

After reviewing the grouped needs, the team should develop a prioritized needs list using a balance of stated user priorities and team member intuition based on user interactions. Decide if a secondary survey is needed to better understand specific needs. Consider if the users' latent needs have been addressed. Discuss what surprises there were and why. Update the User Profile, User Experience and Product Haiku.

USER ANALYSIS

Category	User Statement	Interpreted Need	Specification	Priority
Product uses				
Likes				
Dislikes				
Suggestions				

EXAMPLE - PARENT APP

Category	User Statement	Interpreted Need	Specification	Priority
Product uses	Make set-up easy	Easy to create profile set-up	Intuitive set-up	1
	Search for good match	Relevant search with filters	Search with appropriate filters	1
	Playmates must be close by	Playmates must be in certain locations	Geographic matching	1
	Want to join groups	Group participation	Group creation	2
	Want to post questions	Access to forums	Forum functionality	3
Likes	I like LinkedIn search ease	Easy to create profile set-up	Intuitive set-up	1
	I like the Facebook Groups	Group participation	Group creation	2
Dislikes	I'm worried that personal info will be exposed	Privacy concerns	Privacy firewalls decisions	1
Suggestions	Don't become cluttered like other networks	Clean, intuitive look	Clean GUI	1
	Include kids' interests (sports, games, etc.)	Profile includes kids' interests	Profile with parent and kid areas	1

EXAMPLE - PARENT ADVOCATE

Category	User Statement	Interpreted Need	Specification	Priority
Product uses	I could use help to navigate the school	Need guide on preschool and school	School system introduction	1
	My child might be missing out	Learn about available resources	Provide full resource offering	1
	What should I being doing with my child?	Want training on child learning activities	Child rearing classes	2
	Meet more moms with kids my child's age	Want community introductions	Community events	3
Likes	I want to feel respected	Repsectful and culturally sensitive	Advocate interation protocols	1
Dislikes	I don't trust outsiders	Develop neighborhood relationships	Develop consistent presence	1
	I don't like being told what to do		Advocate interation protocols	1
	I don't want to travel outside my area		Events in neighborhoods	2
Suggestions	Work with people I know	Trust by association	Develop local partnerships	1

EXAMPLE - BIKE DESK

Category	User Statement	Interpreted Need	Specification	Priority
Product uses	I use my bike to exercise while checking email	More bike look and feel	Intergrated bike unit with desk	1
	I use the desk when I am standing and sitting	Adjustable heights	Adjustable height desk/bike	1
Likes	I want a real bike unit	More traditional bike look and feel	Traditional bike seat	1
	I want a real bike seat	More traditional bike look and feel	Bike unit looks more like bike	2
	I want software that tracks my performance	Tracking capability	Bluetooth enabled software	3
Dislikes	I don't like big units	Smaller size area	Small footprint	1
	I don't like fat seats	More traditional bike look and feel	Traditional bike seat	1
	I don't like upright unit	More traditional bike look and feel	Bike unit looks more like bike	2
Suggestions	Make the unit feel solid	Solid construction	Larger size tubing	2

 SWOT Analysis

A SWOT analysis is a great way to understand the environment in which your organization, profit or non-profit will compete. List the organization's strengths and weaknesses which are internal factors. In addition, list the opportunities and threats which are external factors. If your organization is a startup, a SWOT analysis is very important in helping set goals.

| STRENGTH | WEAKNESS |
| OPPORTUNITY | THREAT |

SWOT ANALYSIS	
Strengths	Weaknesses
Opportunities	Threats

EXAMPLE PARENTING APP

Strengths	Weaknesses
Focused niche with clear purpose	No scale
App revenue model	Adoption rate is unclear
High income, motivated user base	
Easy to pilot	
Modest build-out costs	
Great user interface	

Opportunities	Threats
Large urban, suburban areas	Other parenting app with user base enters
Families that are moving	

EXAMPLE PARENTING ADVOCATE

Strengths	Weaknesses
Holistic solution provider	Parents may not buy in
Connect-the-dots solution, many services in place	Other agencies may feel threatened
Strong community ties	Unclear long term funding
Local expertise	School district may not focus on 0-6 year-olds
Leverage off HCZ and EDCI best practices	

Opportunities	Threats
Cooperate with churches and nonprofits	

EXAMPLE BIKE DESK

Strengths	Weaknesses
Can benefit from market segmentation	Not first mover
Take "real cycle" positioning	No distribution
	High minimum order quantities
	Considerable development expenses

Opportunities	Threats
Real cycle unit would be valued	Existing player offers middle price point
Middle price point available	Walking desk companies can enter market
Market to cycling enthusiasts	

Using these research tools correctly can be the difference between your enterprise's success and failure. While everyone agrees in the benefit of doing rigorous research, most do not know how. Even fewer actually do the research. Many aspiring entrepreneurs only do light online research. By actually doing this rigorous research before you start a venture, you can save a great deal of time and money and possibly even avoid unnecessary failure. Remember the existence of competitors validates the idea. Be clear on how your solution is better than theirs.

CONCLUSION
- ✓ Go deep in research
- ✓ Increase success

Improvise

Let's analyze the interview content. The goal is to translate customer needs into product/service features. First, interpret the stated customer needs using the following criteria:

1. Categorize the needs in product uses, likes, dislikes and suggestions

2. Be as specific as possible using affirmative statements, not negative.

3. State what the product can do, not how it will do it or what the product user can do.

4. Include the users' priority when possible.

5. Manage time into 10 or 15 minute sessions and take a 2-3 minute break.

The goal of improvisation is to generate as many potential solutions as you can based on research, particularly user feedback. Be messy. Overshoot on the ideas. Write them down no matter how crazy they may seem. Don't be critical here, just come up with lots of ideas. Editing will happen later. The volume of ideas is more important than the value of ideas at this stage. Divergent thinking, which includes unexpected possibilities, should be the call to action.

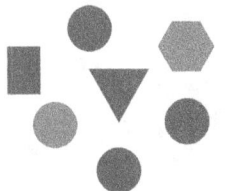

Improvision Needs
1. Good research
2. Great chemistry

Create Twist
1. Yes and...
2. If.. then

How
1. Write down every idea
2. Be messy
3. Overshoot
4. Set 10-15 minute blocks
5. Have fun

 # Instructions

Goal: Develop a crisp version of the Product Haiku

Outcomes: Product/Service Haiku Version 2, Product Specifications and Prototype

Environment: Find an open space with a creative vibe if possible. Have access to blackboards, whiteboards or large tablets of paper, post-its, pens and timer. Warm up with some improvisation exercises. Ideate in 10-15 minute blocks and take 2-3 minute breaks.

Key Steps

1. Create a playful atmosphere by warming up with group games found in Improvise section. Be sure to review the Ideation Rules.

2. Have individual team members briefly recap the User Profile, User Experience, Imagine in 5 years.., Product Haiku and User Analysis.

3. Create an idea sketch with user in the middle. Write as many possible solutions for the user needs using the affirmative on sticky notes or on paper.

4. Fully explore the ideas by using the statements 'Yes and...' or "If...Then..." Avoid "No, but..."

5. When the team gets stuck, ask the question "What if?" to keep going.

6. Another method to get unstuck is to have one team member play the user who explains a mock up in the affirmative for several minutes.

7. When the session has played out, group the ideas into similar categories. Create simple Product Specifications for the most promising 2-3 ideas. Don't be tempted to edit. Send the Product Specifications to the team and let the ideas ferment for some time, 2-7 days ideally.

8. Make a prototype based on the most promising product specifications if possible.

Curate

Curating can be the most frustrating stage, as well as the time where the greatest epiphanies happen. Outcomes can range from absolute epiphany to validation. Epiphany is when the team identifies a completely new way to solve the problem, while validation is confirmation of an already solid idea. Validation is a great result in that the team can feel that they chose the best solution out of all possible solutions. For this reason, don't skimp on this stage.

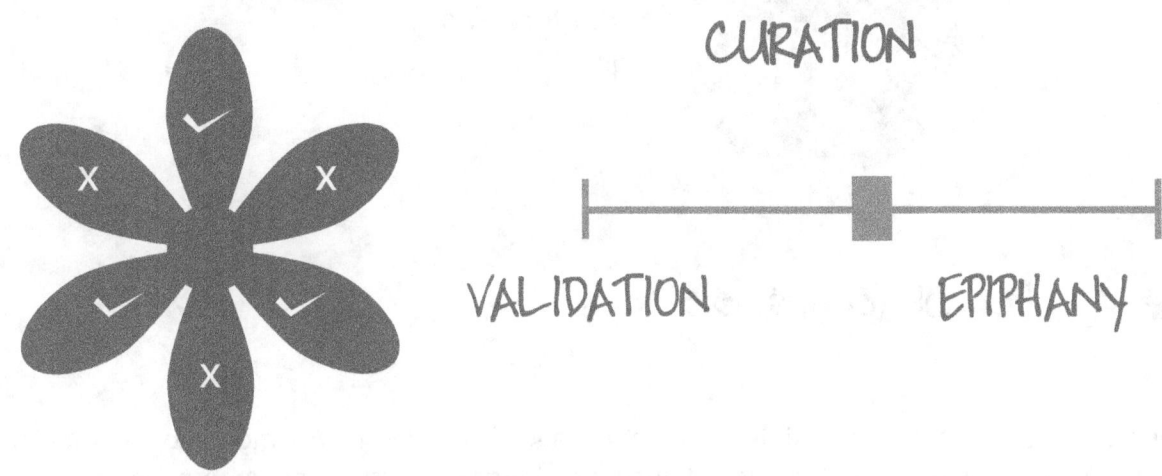

In this stage, revisit the 2-4 ideas from improvisation with a fresh pair of eyes, ideally a few days later. Exercise or do physical activities which allows the subconscious to ponder the ideas. The goal is consider mashing up or remixing the ideas in a group session. In this stage, economic feasibility and team execution capabilities are introduced by developing a rough development cost and economic analysis.

A FEW DAYS LATER....

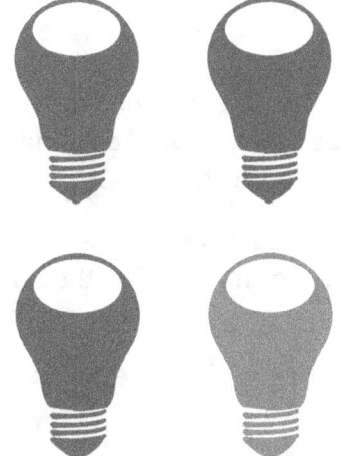

+ Economic analysis
+ Team capability

Ideally, the team is finding ways to get the development costs as low as possible to ensure the feasibility of a new product/service launch. The economic analysis lays out the stark details of potential sales versus product/service costs. For commercial ventures, product/service costs will likely need to be less than 50% of the potential sales. For non-profits, direct service costs and overhead must be less than funds raised.

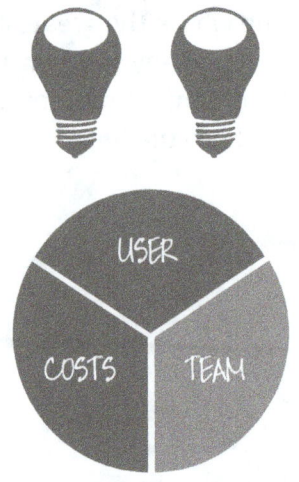

CURATION

How:
1. New Prototype
2. New user and stakeholder interviews
3. Repeat if needed

 Economic Analysis

The purpose of an economic analysis is to answer the age old question, "Will more money come in than out?" If the answer is yes, then there is a chance for a long term sustainable enterprise. If the answer is no, then what can be done to mitigate the need for more money or change the product?

No worries if you don't know the exact numbers; guestimate. Over time, you can refine the numbers. The exercise is a reality check.

Sales can be calculated in the following ways: For product, the easiest way to forecast sales is to multiply the sales price and the # units. For services, sales can be calculated as average service fee multiplied by the number of jobs. For non profits, grants will be the revenues needed to breakeven or run a small surplus.

Expenses can be broken down into several buckets: materials, labor, marketing and other. Development costs, which usually happens in the first few months of an enterprise, are often broken down to materials, design, research, overhead.

The cash flow is determined by sales minus expenses. Total cash uses are cumulative cash uses over several months. This figure determines how much money is needed to start up. Add a buffer as things always take longer than expected and there will always be unexpected costs.

A key question to answer is how much can you charge for your products or services relative to your costs? Are these realistic rates given other options in the market? For non profits, the question is do the services provide significant value compared to the costs?

The purpose of this analysis is to get a rough idea if the economics work.

ECONOMIC ANALYSIS

Month	1	2	3	4	5	6
# Units Sold						
Avg. Sales Price						
Total Sales (# Units x Price)						
Material						
Labor						
Marketing						
Other						
Development						
Total Costs						
Cash Flow						
Total Cash Uses						
Development Costs	$	%				
Development						
Designer						
Research Costs						
Overhead						
Total						
# Development Months						

EXAMPLE - PARENT APP

Month	1	2	3	4	5	6
# Units Sold	300	400	500	700	1,000	1,500
Avg. Sales Price	5	5	5	5	5	5
Total Sales (# Units x Price)	1,500	2,000	2,500	3,500	5,000	7,500
Material						
Labor						
Marketing	5,300	400	500	700	1,000	1,500
Other						
Development	22,000					
Total Costs	27,300	400	500	700	1,000	1,500
Cash Flow	(25,800)	1,600	2,000	2,800	4,000	6,000
Total Cash Uses		(24,200)	(22,200)	(19,400)	(15,400)	(9,400)
Development Costs	$	%				
Development	15,000					
Designer	7,000					
Research Costs						
Overhead						
Total	22,000					
# Development Months	5					

EXAMPLE - PARENT ADVOCATE

Month			1	2	3	4	5	6
# Units Sold			0	0	0	0	0	0
Avg. Sales Price		15,000	5	5	5	5	5	5
Total Sales (# Units x Price)		7,000	0	0	0	0	0	0
Material			0	0	0	0	0	0
Labor		22,000	5,000	5,000	5,000	5,000	5,000	5,000
Marketing		5	0	0	0	0	0	0
Other			1,000	1,000	1,000	1,000	1,000	1,000
Development			0	0	0	0	0	0
Total Costs			6,000	6,000	6,000	6,000	6,000	6,000
Cash Flow			(6,000)	(6,000)	(6,000)	(6,000)	(6,000)	(6,000)
Total Cash Uses				(12,000)	(18,000)	(24,000)	(30,000)	(36,000)
Development Costs			$	%				
Curriculum			15,000					
Labor			0					
Research Costs			0					
Overhead			0					
Total			15,000					
# Development Months			5					

EXAMPLE - BIKE DESK

Month		1	2	3	4	5	6
# Units Sold		350	500	750	800	900	1,000
Avg. Sales Price		900	900	900	900	900	900
Total Sales (# Units x Price)		315,000	450,000	675,000	720,000	810,000	900,000
Material		157,500	225,000	337,500	360,000	405,000	450,000
Labor		20,000	20,000	20,000	20,000	20,000	20,000
Marketing		123,000	120,000	185,000	194,000	212,000	230,000
Other		15,000	15,000	15,000	15,000	15,000	15,000
Development		57,000	0	0	0	0	0
Total Costs		372,500	380,000	557,500	589,000	652,000	715,000
Cash Flow		(57,500)	70,000	117,500	131,000	158,000	185,000
Total Cash Uses			12,500	130,000	261,000	419,000	604,000
Development Costs		$	%				
Curriculum		40,000	70%				
Labor		0	0%				
Research Costs		5,000	9%				
Overhead		12,000	21%				
Total		57,000	100%				
# Development Months		5					

# Instructions

Goal: Narrow options by mashing up the best aspects and introducing economic analysis and stakeholder input

Outcomes: Product/Service Haiku v3, Product Specifications v2 and Prototype v2, Economic Analysis v1 and Stakeholder Analysis v1

Environment: Find an open space with a creative vibe if possible. Have access to blackboards, whiteboards or large tablets of paper, post-its, pens and timer. Warm up with some improvisation exercises.

Key Steps

1. Revisit the top 3-4 choices as a team. Try to combine best aspects if possible.

2. Conduct a preliminary economic analysis which includes development costs and ongoing economic analysis.

3. Validate the product/service by completing user and stakeholder surveys. Use the latest prototype if possible.

4. Update User Profile, Experience and Product Haiku if necessary.

5. Repeat the curate process as many times as needed.

The edit stage entails making final tradeoffs between user needs, cost and capabilities. As a group, review the new user and stakeholder analysis and latest economic analysis. Using the rules of editing, develop a team consensus on the final product/service specifications.

Finalize the Product Haiku and complete detailed product/service specifications. Update the user profile and user experience if necessary. Finally, develop a presentation that summarizes the team's findings.

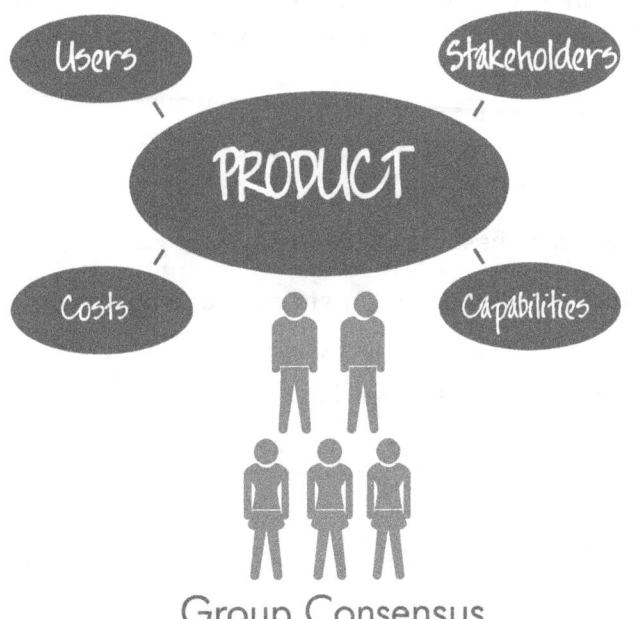

How:

1. Finalize tradeoffs
2. Complete haiku and specs
3. Update user profile / and experience
4. Develop presentation

Goal: Make final tradeoffs for finished Product Haiku and Product Specifications and prototype

Outcomes: Product/Service Haiku Final, Product Specifications Final and Prototype Final, Economic Analysis Final

Environment: Find an open space with a creative vibe if possible. Have access to blackboards, whiteboards or large tablets of paper, post-its, pens and timer. Warm up with some improvisation exercises.

Key Steps

1. Make final decisions on product/service specifications.

2. Develop presentation to communicate summarized findings to stakeholders.

# PRESENTATION

The Presentation consolidates the key lessons of the design thinking process. The document clarifies positions amongst the team. In addition, it is an excellent communication tool for people outside of the team including management, stakeholders and employees.

In the template, most pages are comprised of charts created during the design thinking process. Copy those charts into the template and add conclusions. Personalize the presentation by adding visuals and changing layout. Feel free to add more slides if more detail helps. Be sure the visual presentation fully represents the efforts of the team.

Use the Google Presentati on template found at http://tinyurl.com/nttxcx8

More detailed instructions are found in the notes section of the presentation.

Presentation Template

(Add image)

(NAME)

PRODUCT DEFINTION

(DATE)

FEATURES COMPARISON

- Key features include XXXX.

FEATURES COMPARISON			
Company:			
Key Benefit			
Price			
Features			
Advantages			
Shortcomings			

CUSTOMER PROFILE

(Add Graphic)　　(Add Graphic)

CUSTOMER PROFILE - Create by filling out below	Customer 1	Customer 2
Name		
Age range		
Gender		
Most important benefits they care about		
How important is price?		
How they research the product		
Where they buy		
When they buy (impulse, long research, seasonal)		
Is it a repeat buy? If so, what is the pattern?		
Adjacent products? (think toothbrush and toothpaste)		
Which competitor product do they use?		
Average Units Purchased Guesstimate		
Average Price Guesstimate		
Average Purchase Amount Guesstimate		
Average Marketing Investment Guesstimate		
Percentage Marketing / Purchasing (2-30%)		

USER NEEDS ANALYSIS

- Key needs include XXXX.

USER NEEDS ANALYSIS				
Category	User Statement	Interpreted Need	Specification	Priority
Product uses				
Likes				
Dislikes				
Suggestions				

(Add photo/graphic)

DESCRIPTION & KEY BENEFIT

Description
- (Add 10-15 word description)

Key Benefit
- (Add 10-15 word description)

PRODUCT HAIKU

PRODUCT HAIKU		distill more to less...
Problem		
User	1	
	2	
	3	
Stakeholders	1	
	2	
	3	
Constraints	1	
	2	
	3	
	4	
	5	
Solution		
Key benefits	1	
	2	
	3	
Features	1	
	2	
	3	
	4	
	5	
How different?		
Price estimate?		
Development cost?		
Next steps	1	
	2	
	3	
	4	
	5	

CUSTOMER EXPERIENCE

Awareness

(Add text and graphics)

How & Where Buy

(Add text and graphics)

If there is a problem

(Add text and graphics)

ONLINE RESEARCH

Conclusions

- Takeaway 1
- Takeaway 2
- Takeaway 3

Product/Service Competitors	
Name	Website
Name	Website
Name	Website

SWOT ANALYSIS

Strengths	Weaknesses
Opportunities	Threats

KEY LEARNINGS

Experts
- Takeaway 1
- Takeaway 2
- Takeaway 3

Stakeholders
- Takeaway 1
- Takeaway 2
- Takeaway 3

ECONOMIC ANALYSIS

- Key points include XXXX.

ECONOMIC ANALYSIS						
Month	1	2	3	4	5	6
# Units Sold						
Avg. Sales Price						
Total Sales (# Units x Price)						
Material						
Labor						
Marketing						
Other						
Development						
Total Costs						
Cash Flow						
Total Cash Uses						

Development Costs	$	%
Development		
Designer		
Research Costs		
Overhead		
Total		
# Development Months		

(Add image)

GREAT START PARENT ADVOCATE
PRODUCT DEFINTION
Fall 2015

(Add photo/graphic)

DESCRIPTION & KEY BENEFIT

<u>Description</u>
- Parent Advocate promotes parenting best practices to low wealth parents to eliminate achievement gap.

<u>Key Benefit</u>
- Give low wealth parents peace of mind by providing parenting solutions in culturally sensitive way

CUSTOMER PROFILE

(Add Graphic)   (Add Graphic)

EXAMPLE - PARENT ADVOCATE

Education consultant for low-wealth parents	Customer 1	Customer 2
Name	Low-wealth parents of children 0-6 yrs old	School principals and social workers
Age range	16-35	22-60
Gender	Female	Female
Most important benefits they care about	Respect; What is good for kids and community	Easy to work with and reduce achievement gap
How important is price?	NA	NA
How they research the product	Word-of-mounth	Information sessions
Where they buy	In neighborhood	Information sessions
When they buy (impulse, long research, seasonal)	After hearing from friends and attending sessions	Information sessions
Is it a repeat buy? If so, what is the pattern?	NA	NA
Adjacent products? (think toothbrush and toothpaste)	Preschool, babysitters, county services	Other nonprofits
Which competitor product do they use?	NA	Other nonprofits
Average Units Purchased Guesstimate	NA	NA
Average Price Guesstimate	NA	NA
Average Purchase Amount Guesstimate	NA	NA
Average Marketing Investment Guesstimate	NA	NA
Percentage Marketing / Purchasing (2-30%)	NA	NA

CUSTOMER EXPERIENCE

Awareness

Denise is a 23 year old single mother who has a 3 year old boy and 1 year old girl. She lives in low income housing in the neighborhood in which she grew up.

Denise realizes that her children may be missing out, but she does not trust the system or schools and does not want outsiders telling her what to do.

How & Where Buy

Denise sees a brochure about a local parent advocate. Her friend, Shelia, says that she has joined the program which offers home visits from a parent advocate and classes.

It turns out that the parent advocate is Jennae, who grew up in the neighborhood.

If there is a problem

Denise sets up a home visit where Jennae talks about the program, classes and events. Jennae says she will help navigate the preschool, school system and social services. Jennae emphasizes that she will explain the resources available such as parenting classes at the local school. Denise can make the decision on whether to attend.

If there is a miscommunication between Denise and the parent advocate, Denise can talk to trainers at the classes. After some thought, Denise decides to join her friend Shelia for this week's class.

PRODUCT HAIKU

PRODUCT HAIKU	EXAMPLE - PARENT ADVOCATE
Problem	Achievement gap established when kids are 0-6 years old
User	16-35 year old, low-wealth parents and their kids
	Schools and school district
Stakeholders	1. Schools and school district
	2. State/county youth services
	3. Nonprofits
Constraints	Current solution is Swiss cheese; gaps in key areas
	Parents are suspicious of outside parties
	School district focused on K-12, not preschool
	Preschools don't have resources to deal outside the walls
Solution	Parent Advocate promotes best practices in culturally sensitive way
Key benefits	1. Give parents access to best practices
	2. Build community and awareness of local kids resources
	3. Help school district better understand incoming students
Features	1. Parent meetings to learn about resources
	2. In-house family visits
	3. Local resource mapping guide
	4. Best practices curriculum for parents and kids
	5. Organized playdates at schools and parks
How different?	Incomplete network in local communities
Price	NA
How to develop & cost?	Curriculum Dev: $15K, Advocates $50K x 1 in Phase 1
Next steps	1. Garner stakeholder support
	2. Develop curriculum
	3. Recruit advocates
	4. Pilot program
	5

ONLINE RESEARCH

Conclusions

- Most other programs don't have enough data to make conclusions.
- HCZ and EDCI would be great resources.
- Much activity in this space.

EXAMPLE - PARENT ADVOCATE

Product/Service Competitors

Name	Website
Harlem Children's Zone	http://hcz.org
Great resource. They don't have much experience on 0-6 year olds. A real model for holistic solution. Great way to see pitfalls based on their expereinces. Their Baby College and Harlem Gems programs are most relevant.	
East Durham Children's Initative	http://edci.org
Developing early childhood initiative. Very friendly staff. Great to get some benchmarking.	
Head Start of Lane County	http://www.hsolc.org
Great job descriptions and metrics. Contact staff to better understand their experiences.	

FEATURES COMPARISON

- Key features include classes, in-house visits & school help.

EXAMPLE - PARENTING ADVOCATE

Company:	Parenting Advocate	Harlem Childrens Zone	EDCI
Key Benefit	Reduce achievement gap	Reduce achievement gap	Reduce achievement gap
	Parent support	Parent support	Parent support
	Kids get equal opportunity	Kids get equal opportunity	Kids get equal opportunity
	Build community	Build community	Build community
Price	NA	NA	NA
Features	Parent cheerleader	Parent cheerleader	Parent cheerleader
	Parenting classes	Parenting classes	Parenting classes
	In-home visits	In-home visits	In-home visits
	Partner with school	Truly holistic support	Almost holistic support
		Graduate to next program	Graduate to next program
		Fully integrated with school	Partner with school
Advantages	Smaller target group	Well funded	Well funded
Shortcomings	Phased approach	Big urban challenges	Urban challenges
	Less funding		

Notes: Our program can learn from the experiences and offerings of HCZ and EDCI. Our target audience is much smaller and the community has comparatively more resources though the program does not.

SWOT ANALYSIS

EXAMPLE - PARENTING ADVOCATE

Strengths	Weaknesses
Holistic solution provider	Parents may not buy in
Connect-the-dots solution, many services in place	Other agencies may feel threatened
Strong community ties	Unclear long term funding
Local expertise	School district may not focus on 0-6 year-olds
Leverage off HCZ and EDCI best practices	
Opportunities	**Threats**
Cooperate with churches and nonprofits	

KEY LEARNINGS

Experts
- Parents want what is best for their kids, as they define "best." Knowledge of what services are available is helpful.
- School district, county services, nonprofits. Each has its own mission and metrics.
- It will be very hard to walk the fine line of providing help and respecting the culture. Community and school buy-in will be key. Realize other issues will arise.

Stakeholders
- I really like the concept of reducing the achievement gap before they join the district.
- The achievement gap has not changed in our district for 25 years. We need to try something different.
- Users have low trust levels for outsiders. It will take time to build relationships.

USER NEEDS ANALYSIS

- Key needs include trust, school navigation help, and classes.

EXAMPLE - PARENT ADVOCATE

Category	User Statement	Interpreted Need	Specification	Priority
Product uses	I could use help to navigate the school	Need guide on preschool and school	School system introduction	1
	My child might be missing out	Learn about available resources	Provide full resource offering	1
	What should I being doing with my child?	Want training on child learning activities	Child rearing classes	2
	Meet more moms with kids my child's age	Want community introductions	Community events	3
Likes	I want to feel respected	Respectful and culturally sensitive	Advocate interation protocols	1
Dislikes	I don't trust outsiders	Develop neighborhood relationships	Develop consistent presence	1
	I don't like being told what to do		Advocate interation protocols	1
	I don't want to travel outside my area		Events in neighborhoods	2
Suggestions	Work with people I know	Trust by association	Develop local partnerships	1

ECONOMIC ANALYSIS

- Pilot needs $40K development costs and 6 months.

EXAMPLE - PARENT ADVOCATE

Month	1	2	3	4	5	6
# Units Sold	0	0	0	0	0	0
Avg. Sales Price	5	5	5	5	5	5
Total Sales (# Units x Price)	0	0	0	0	0	0
Material	0	0	0	0	0	0
Labor	5,000	5,000	5,000	5,000	5,000	5,000
Marketing	0	0	0	0	0	0
Other	1,000	1,000	1,000	1,000	1,000	1,000
Development	0	0	0	0	0	0
Total Costs	6,000	6,000	6,000	6,000	6,000	6,000
Cash Flow	(6,000)	(6,000)	(6,000)	(6,000)	(6,000)	(6,000)
Total Cash Uses	(6,000)	(12,000)	(18,000)	(24,000)	(30,000)	(36,000)

Development Costs	$	%
Curriculum	15,000	100%
Labor	0	
Research Costs	0	
Overhead	0	
Total	15,000	
# Development Months	5	

(Add image)

PLAYDATE MATCH
PRODUCT DEFINTION
SPRING 2015

(Add photo/graphic)

DESCRIPTION & KEY BENEFIT

Description
- An app which matches compatible kids as well as their compatible parents

Key Benefit)
- Parents have confidence about playdate and that other parents are compatible with them

---

PRODUCT HAIKU

PRODUCT HAIKU	EXAMPLE - PARENTING APP
Problem	Parents want to set up playdates with great kids and parents
User	28-55 year old parents with 2-16 yr old kids
	13-17 year old kids
Stakeholders	1. Parents/Kids
	2. Companies who sell kids/parenting products
	3
Constraints	Parents are time constrained; want ease of use
	Parents spend much time with the parents of the kids' friends
	Hard to find good match of kids to kids and parents to parents
Solution	A match.com/linkedin.com for kid's playdates
Key benefits	1. Parents enjoy spending time with other great parents
	2. Kids are happy to play with likeable matches
	3. Find great kid-related businesses
Features	1. Easy-to-build profile builder
	2. Easy search
	3. Create communities
	4. Share parenting advice
	5. Ratings on kid-related businesses
How different?	No other competitors
Price	$2.99-$9.99
How to develop & cost?	Designer ($7K) Pilot app ($15K)
Next steps	1. Hire graphic designer after developing design brief
	2. Select web developer
	3. Identify pilot area
	4. Develop marketing plan
	5

CUSTOMER PROFILE

(Add Graphic)   (Add Graphic)

EXAMPLE - PLAYDATE APP LinkedIn meets match.com for kids playdates	Customer 1	Customer 2
Name	Parents of 3-14-year-old kids	Kids
Age range	30-55	3-14
Gender	Female mostly	Female Mostly
Most important benefits they care about	Background info on other kids and parents	Background info on other kids
How important is price?	$4.99-$9.99	No more than $9.99
How they research the product	Look online and word-of-mouth	Word of mouth
Where they buy	iTunes or Android	iTunes or Android
When they buy (impulse, long research, seasonal)	Impulse	Impulse
Is it a repeat buy? If so, what is the pattern?	No	No
Adjacent products? (think toothbrush and toothpaste)	LinkedIn	LinkedIn
Which competitor product do they use?	LinkedIn and Facebook	Facebook
Average Units Purchased Guesstimate	1	1
Average Price Guesstimate	$10	$10
Average Purchase Amount Guesstimate	$1	$1
Average Marketing Investment Guesstimate	$2	$2
Percentage Marketing / Purchasing (2-30%)	20%	20%

CUSTOMER EXPERIENCE

Awareness

Samantha is a 38 year old mother of two: Eli, who is 3 years old, and Alexi, who is 6 years old. They live in an apartment and have some playdates but other kids and their families often have their own plans.

In addition, Samantha's husband Steve does not click with the fathers of Eli's and Alexi's friends.

How & Where Buy

Samantha hears about the parent app from a college friend who lives in another city. Samantha had seen some Google Adwords when she did parenting searches but did not click on any. She goes on the App Store and reads the reviews. Though she has concerns about the number of local matches, she buys it anyway as it is only $4.99.

If there is a problem

The app crashed often so she visited the app website and filed a complaint. Within 3 hours, she received a friendly email with a checklist of potential solutions and a telephone number to call if those did not work.

She realized her iOS needed to be updated and afterwards, the app worked fine. She was ready to start using the app.

ONLINE RESEARCH

Conclusions

- No existing competitors
- Emulate match.com and linkedin.com layout
- More research needed in social network development

EXAMPLE - PARENTING APP	
Product/Service Competitors	
Name	Website
Match	www.match.com
Great user interface, emulate their functionality, particularly search features	
Name	Website
LinkedIn	www.linkedin.com
Strong profile information and easy serach. Really good "people also viewed" feature	
Name	Website
eHarmony	www.eHarmony.com
Have some additional functionality and a slightly different search feature	

FEATURES COMPARISON

- Key features include easy-to-use profile builder, search and group creation.

EXAMPLE - PARENTING APP			
Company:	Parenting App	Facebook	LinkedIn
Key Benefit	Learn about other parents	Connect with others	Great profiles
	Learn about other kids' likes	Massive community	Easy search
	Build community		Great for career
	Meet new friends outside circle		
Price	$2.99-$9.99	Free	Free/Premium
Features	Profile builder	Profile builder	Profile builder
	Search features	Search features	Search features
	Create groups	Create groups	Create groups
		Follow friends	Follow friends
Advantages	Niche focused	Massive scale	Massive scale
		Great features	Great features
Shortcomings	Needs to scale	No playdate focus	No playdate focus

Notes: There are great social networks but there is not one with the specific goal of finding good matches for parents to other like-minded parents and kids with other like-minded kids. Facebook and LinkedIn are best of breed and we can identify best functions from their sites and apply to our own.

SWOT ANALYSIS

PARENTING APP

Strengths	Weaknesses
Focused niche with clear purpose	No scale
App revenue model	Adoption rate is unclear
High income, motivated user base	
Easy to pilot	
Modest build-out costs	
Great user interface	

Opportunities	Threats
Large urban, suburban areas	Other parenting app with user base enters
Families that are moving	

KEY LEARNINGS

Experts

- Parents want great playmates for their kids and want to spend time with parents with similar values.

- Is the information trustworthy and will I have sufficient privacy?

- Primary market is urban, higher income families.

Stakeholders

- We are always looking for highly targeted audience platforms.

- Must scale at the local level to prosper and scale at the national level for us to get interested.

- Parents ideally would like to spend time with other cool parents assuming their kids get along.

USER NEEDS ANALYSIS

- Key needs include 1) Make set up easy, 2) Relevant search and
3) Group creation.

Category	User Statement	Interpreted Need	Specification	Priority
Product uses	Make set-up easy	Easy to create profile set-up	Intuitive set-up	1
	Search for good match	Relevant search with filters	Search with appropriate filters	1
	Playmates must be close by	Playmates must be in certain locations	Geographic matching	1
	Want to join groups	Group participation	Group creation	2
	Want to post questions	Access to forums	Forum functionality	3
Likes	I like LinkedIn search ease	Easy to create profile set-up	Intuitive set-up	1
	I like the Facebook Groups	Group participation	Group creation	2
Dislikes	I'm worried that personal info will be exp	Privacy concerns	Privacy firewalls decisions	1
Suggestions	Don't become cluttered like other network	Clean, intuitive look	Clean GUI	1
	Include kids' interests (sports, games, e	Profile includes kids' interests	Profile with parent and kid areas	1

EXAMPLE - PARENT APP

ECONOMIC ANALYSIS

- Development costs of $22K, breakeven in month 2, and payback in month 8.

EXAMPLE - PARENT APP

Month	1	2	3	4	5	6
# Units Sold	300	400	500	700	1,000	1,500
Avg. Sales Price	5	5	5	5	5	5
Total Sales (# Units x Price)	1,500	2,000	2,500	3,500	5,000	7,500
Material						
Labor						
Marketing	5,300	400	500	700	1,000	1,500
Other						
Development	22,000					
Total Costs	27,300	400	500	700	1,000	1,500
Cash Flow	(25,800)	1,600	2,000	2,800	4,000	6,000
Total Cash Uses		(24,200)	(22,200)	(19,400)	(15,400)	(9,400)

Development Costs	$	%
Development	15,000	
Designer	7,000	
Research Costs		
Overhead		
Total	22,000	
# Development Months	5	

(Add image)

WRITE BIKE
PRODUCT DEFINTION
Spring 2016

(Add photo/graphic)

DESCRIPTION & KEY BENEFIT

Description
- Exercise bike and desk combination

Key Benefit
- Get healthy by cycling and working at same time

PRODUCT HAIKU

PRODUCT HAIKU	EXAMPLE - BIKE DESK
Problem	Want to excercise while working at desk
User	White collar workers
	Cycling enthusiasts
Stakeholders	1. Office equipment sellers and cycling bloggers
	2. Manufacturer
	3. Distribution
Constraints	Move and scale to market quickly
	Easy to assemble
	Small footprint
Solution	Desk with integrated bike
Key benefits	1. Great health and cycling benefits
	2. Peace of mind
Features	1. Solid feel to bike
	2. Smooth and quiet operating
	3. Easy to assemble
	4. Metric software
	5
How different?	Options at attractive price point
Price	$900
How to develop & cost?	$10K development
Next steps	1. Develop design brief and prototype
	2. Determine manufacturer
	3. Find distribution partner
	4. Create marketing collateral
	5

CUSTOMER PROFILE

(Add Graphic)   (Add Graphic)

EXAMPLE - BIKE DESK	Customer 1	Customer 2
Name	White collar workers	Cycling enthusiasts
Age range	30-60	35-60
Gender	Male	Male
Most important benefits they care about	Get healthy	Get extra ride time
How important is price?	$300-$1,000	$600-$1,500
How they research the product	Look online but want to see before buying	Look online but want to see before buying
Where they buy	Office furniture store or online	Office furniture store or online
When they buy (impulse, long research, seasonal)	Long research mostly	Long research mostly
Is it a repeat buy? If so, what is the pattern?	No	No
Adjacent products? (think toothbrush and toothpaste)	Office furniture	Office furniture and bike shops
Which competitor product do they use?	LifeSpan	LifeSpan
Average Units Purchased Guesstimate	1	1
Average Price Guesstimate	$900	$1,200
Average Purchase Amount Guesstimate	$1,100	$1,500
Average Marketing Investment Guesstimate	$90	$1,200
Percentage Marketing / Purchasing (2-30%)	10%	10%

CUSTOMER EXPERIENCE

Awareness

Chris is a 43 year old graphic designer who works from home. After his physician recommended that he lose weight, Chris started riding a bicycle. He really liked how some of his most creative ideas happened when he was riding.

How & Where Buy

Even though he'd seen AdWords for the Write Cycle Desk, Christian only became interested when he saw a short *Bicycling* magazine article about the desk. Christian bought the product online, especially because of the 100% money back guarantee including freight.

He considered the desk-only option, but then thought an upright indoor bike/desk combination worked best for him. Christian reasoned that he would not be able able to do heavy graphic design on the Bike Desk, but he could read, answer emails and make Skype calls.

The Write Bike Desk would not replace outdoor cycling but it would be a good way to build aerobic activity, particularly on rainy days.

If there is a problem

Chris found the seat uncomfortable and had a question on how to adjust the handlebar height. He visited the website and watched videos on handlebar height adjustment.

Chris called the company and left a voicemail. Within 4 hours, a customer service rep called back and offered several options for seats. Chris was pleased with his experience so far.

ONLINE RESEARCH

Conclusions

- Market segmentation already.
- Lots of low price-point product.
- Gap in middle price-point.

EXAMPLE - BIKE DESK

Product/Service Competitors

Name	Website
LifeSpan Fitness	http://www.lifespanfitness.com
First mover with good looking product. Category leader. Higher price point and untested cycling unit.	

Name	Website
Desk Cycle	http://deskcycle.com
Very inexpensive under existing desk unit.	

Name	Website
Sunny Desk Cycle	http://sunnydeskcycle.com
Really cheap pedaling-only units.	

FEATURES COMPARISON

- Key features include adjustable desk, easy assembly & storage.

EXAMPLE - BIKE DESK

Company:	LifeSpan Fitness	DeskCycle	Sunny Desk Cycle
Key Benefit	Excercise while you work	Excercise while you work	Excercise while you work
Price	$1,100	$160	$49
Features	Adjustable desk	Quiet magnetic resistance	Dial in resistance
	Matching bike unit	Low height	Portable unit
	Tracking software	5 function display	
	Small footprint		
Advantages	Modular system	Compact unit	Cheap
	Good distribution	Easy to store	Small unit
Shortcomings	High price	Not real cycling unit	Not real cycling unit
	Insufficient cycle for enthusiasts		Questionable quality

Notes: The gaps are a well-made product that has a solid cycling unit at a middle price point. Software would be a nice add-on feature. The low end of the market is saturated.

SWOT ANALYSIS

EXAMPLE - BIKE DESK

Strengths	Weaknesses
Can benefit from market segmentation Take "real cycle" positioning	Not first mover No distribution High minimum order quantities Considerable development expenses
Opportunities	**Threats**
Real cycle unit would be valued Middle price point available Market to cycling enthusiasts	Existing player offers middle price point Walking desk companies can enter market

KEY LEARNINGS

Experts
- Overall category is continuing to grow 20%+ annually. Appealing to office workers and cycling enthusiasts may be tough. May need to focus on one segment first.
- Distribution is key while Minimum Order Quantities will be big issue with manufacturers.

Stakeholders
- Cycling unit can be made to feel solid.
- Lead time of 20 weeks and minimum order quantities of 10,000 units.
- Heavier gauge tubing and belt drive for easier maintenance.

USER NEEDS ANALYSIS

- Key needs include real bike unit with real bike seat.

EXAMPLE - BIKE DESK

Category	User Statement	Interpreted Need	Specification	Priority
Product uses	Use bike to exercise while checking email	More bike look and feel	Intergrated bike unit with desk	1
	Use desk when I am standing and sitting	Adjustable heights	Adjustable height desk/bike	1
Likes	I want a real bike unit	More traditional bike look and feel	Traditional bike seat	1
	I want a real bike seat	More traditional bike look and feel	Bike unit looks more like bike	2
	I want software that tracks my performance	Tracking capability	Bluetooth enabled software	3
Dislikes	I don't like big units	Smaller size area	Small footprint	1
	I don't like fat seats	More traditional bike look and feel	Traditional bike seat	1
	I don't like upright unit	More traditional bike look and feel	Bike unit looks more like bike	2
Suggestions	Make the unit feel solid	Solid construction	Larger size tubing	2

ECONOMIC ANALYSIS

- Pilot needs $40K development costs and 6 months.

EXAMPLE - PARENT ADVOCATE

Month	1	2	3	4	5	6
# Units Sold	0	0	0	0	0	0
Avg. Sales Price	5	5	5	5	5	5
(illegible)	0	0	0	0	0	0
Material	0	0	0	0	0	0
Labor	5,000	5,000	5,000	5,000	5,000	5,000
Marketing	0	0	0	0	0	0
Other	1,000	1,000	1,000	1,000	1,000	1,000
Development	0	0	0	0	0	0
Total Costs	6,000	6,000	6,000	6,000	6,000	6,000
Cash Flow	(6,000)	(6,000)	(6,000)	(6,000)	(6,000)	(6,000)
Total Cash Uses	(6,000)	(12,000)	(18,000)	(24,000)	(30,000)	(36,000)

Development Costs	$	%
Curriculum	15,000	100%
Labor	0	
Research Costs	0	
Overhead	0	
Total	15,000	
# Development Months	6	

TOOLKIT

This toolkit is ideal to use once you understand the design thinking concepts. Review the map to familiarize yourself with tools in each area of the PRICE method. Use the checklist and fill out the templates as you apply the design thinking process. The templates are also available online for download. Refer back to previous sections if you need help in reacquainting yourself with the concepts. The parenting app example is also included for reference.

In a group setting, start with a couple of warm up exercises to get the team on the same page. Over time, experiment with the different exercises to find best combinations for your group. At the first session, try the Turning Point exercise after a couple of warm up exercises. This will quickly help build group rapport

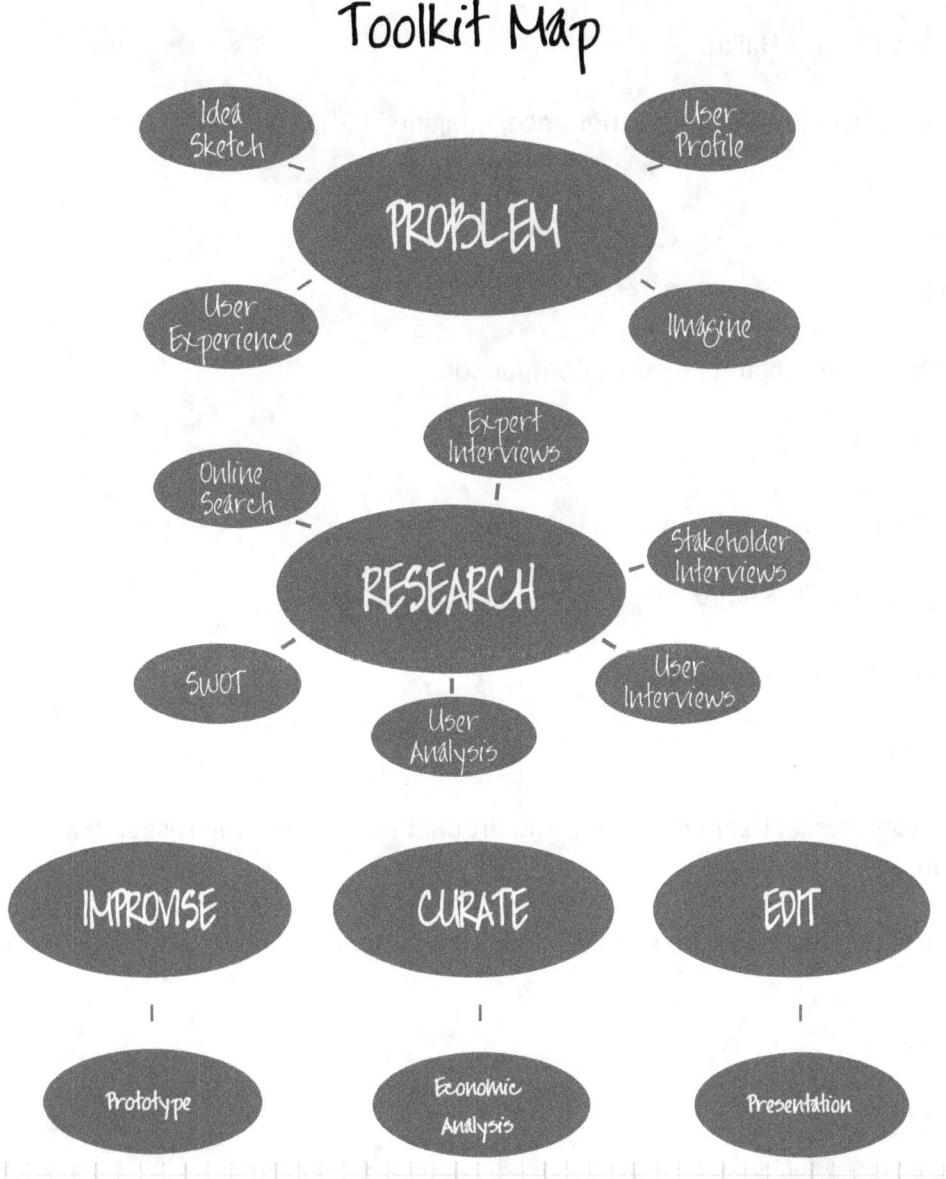

CHECKLIST

PROBLEM

- [ ] Draw out an idea sketch.

- [ ] Complete a user profile.

- [ ] Write out a user experience.

- [ ] Complete an "Imagine in 5 years…" sketch.

- [ ] Reconcile the idea sketch, user profile and customer experience so that they are consistent.

- [ ] Complete the Product Haiku.

Tools: Idea Sketch, User Profile, User Experience, Imagine in 5 Years

RESEARCH

- [ ] Complete Online Search and Features Comparison.

- [ ] Initiate expert interviews.

- [ ] Complete stakeholders interviews.

- [ ] Conduct user needs discovery.

- [ ] Complete user needs taxonomy.

- [ ] Create SWOT analysis.

- [ ] Revisit the User Profile, User Experience and Product Haiku given the research and user needs and needs taxonomy.

Tools: Features, Expert Interview, Stakeholder Interviews User Interviews, User Analysis, SWOT, features

IMPROVISE

- [ ] Generate as many possible solutions.
- [ ] Make a prototype.
- [ ] Revisit the User Profile, User Experience and Product Haiku.

CURATE

- [ ] Develop an economic analysis.
- [ ] Mashup ideas and narrow options down.
- [ ] Conduct secondary user interviews if necessary.
- [ ] Revise prototype.
- [ ] Update User Profile, Experience and Product Haiku.
- [ ] Repeat Curate process as needed.

Tools: Cost Analysis

EDIT

- [ ] Finalize Economic Analysis.
- [ ] Make final tradeoffs.
- [ ] Complete product/service specifications.
- [ ] Develop presentation.

Tools: Presentation

TEMPLATES
Problem

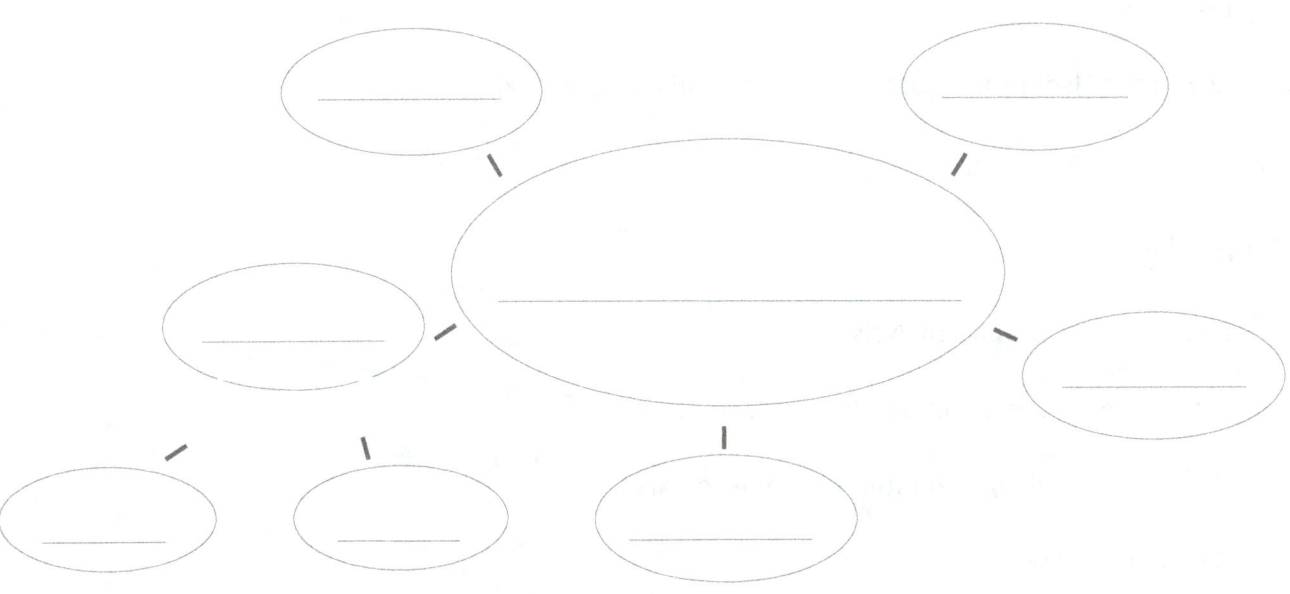

CUSTOMER PROFILE		
Name	Customer 1	Customer 2
Age range		
Gender		
Most important benefits they care about		
How important is price?		
How they research the product		
Where they buy		
When they buy (impulse, long research, seasonal)		
Is it a repeat buy? If so, what is the pattern?		
Adjacent products? (think toothbrush and toothpaste)		
Which competitor product do they use?		
Average Units Purchased Guesstimate		
Average Price Guesstimate		
Average Purchase Amount Guesstimate		
Average Marketing Investment Guesstimate		
Percentage Marketing / Purchasing (2-30%)		

CUSTOMER EXPERIENCE
1. Who is the customer?
2. How did they become aware of the product/service?
3. Where and how do they purchase/join the product/service?
4. What happens is there is a problem?
Note: Use a word document if you prefer.

Imagine in 5 Years...

PRODUCT HAIKU		
Problem		
User	1	
	2	
	3	
Stakeholders	1	
	2	
	3	
Constraints	1	
	2	
	3	
	4	
	5	
Solution		
Key benefits	1	
	2	
	3	
Features	1	
	2	
	3	
	4	
	5	
How different?		
Price estimate?		
Develop cost?		
Next steps	1	
	2	
	3	
	4	
	5	

ONLINE RESEARCH

Product/Service Competitors		Relevant Experts			
Name	Website	Name	Contact	Website	Email Phone
Comment					
Name	Website	Relevant Associations			
		Title	Contact	Website	Email Phone
Comment					
		Relevant Research & Publications Title			
		Title	Website		
Name	Website				
Comment					
Name	Website				
Comment					

FEATURES COMPARISON				
Company:				
Key Benefit				
Price				
Features				
Advantages				
Shortcomings				

EXPERT INTERVIEWS
Customer |于

What is your opinion of the product/service?

What key benefits are users seeking?

What is the secondary market for this product/service?

What assumptions and constraints do you see in the user base?

Who are the key stakeholders and what are their needs?

When and why do individuals use this kind of product/service?

What do users enjoy about current products?

What do users not like about current products?

What are the key issues before users select?

What improvements do you suggest?

STAKEHOLDER INTERVIEWS
Manufacturer
How would you like to see the product/service improve?
What are your key constraints?
What are your key organization's needs?
What do you not like about current products?
What improvements do you suggest?
What are the key benefits that the user is seeking?
What is the primary market for this product/service?
What is the secondary market for this product/service?
What assumptions and constraints do you see in the user base?

USER INTERVIEWS

When and why do you use this kind of product/service?

Explain how you use the product

What do you enjoy about current products?

What do you dislike about current products?

What are the key issues when buying?

What improvements do you suggest?

What are the most important points we should understand?

Note:

Remember:

Position yourself as researcher rather than owner.

Clearly define the user.

Let go of preconceived notions.

Determine user priorities.

Be aware of latent needs.

USER ANALYSIS

Category	User Statement	Interpreted Need	Specification	Priority
Product uses				
Likes				
Dislikes				
Suggestions				

SWOT ANALYSIS

Strengths	Weaknesses

Opportunities	Threats

Curate

ECONOMIC ANALYSIS						
Month	1	2	3	4	5	6
# Units Sold						
Avg. Sales Price						
Total Sales (# Units x Price)						
Material						
Labor						
Marketing						
Other						
Development						
Total Costs						
Cash Flow						
Total Cash Uses						
Development Costs	$	%				
Development						
Designer						
Research Costs						
Overhead						
Total						
# Development Months						

Edit

(NAME)
PRODUCT DEFINTION
(DATE)

(Add image)

(Add photo/graphic)

DESCRIPTION & KEY BENEFIT

Description
- (Add 10-15 word description)

Key Benefit
- (Add 10-15 word description)

PRODUCT HAIKU

PRODUCT HAIKU — distill more to less...

- Problem
- User (1, 2, 3)
- Stakeholders (1, 2, 3)
- Constraints (1, 2, 3, 4, 5)
- Solution
- Key benefits (1, 2, 3)
- Features (1, 2, 3, 4, 5)
- How different?
- Price estimate?
- Development cost?
- Next steps (1, 2, 3, 4, 5)

CUSTOMER PROFILE

(Add Graphic)   (Add Graphic)

CUSTOMER PROFILE – Create by filling out below

	Customer 1	Customer 2
Name		
Age range		
Gender		
Most important benefits they care about		
How important is price?		
How they research the product		
Where they buy		
When they buy (impulse, long research, seasonal)		
Is it a repeat buy? If so, what is the pattern?		
Adjacent products? (think toothbrush and toothpaste)		
Which competitor product do they use?		
Average Units Purchased Guesstimate		
Average Price Guesstimate		
Average Purchase Amount Guesstimate		
Average Marketing Investment Guesstimate		
Percentage Marketing / Purchasing (2-30%)		

CUSTOMER EXPERIENCE

Awareness

(Add text and graphics)

How & Where Buy

(Add text and graphics)

If there is a problem

(Add text and graphics)

ONLINE RESEARCH

Conclusions

- Takeaway 1
- Takeaway 2
- Takeaway 3

Product/Service Competitors

Name	Website

Name	Website

Name	Website

FEATURES COMPARISON

- Key features include XXXX.

SWOT ANALYSIS

KEY LEARNINGS

Experts
- Takeaway 1
- Takeaway 2
- Takeaway 3

Stakeholders
- Takeaway 1
- Takeaway 2
- Takeaway 3

USER NEEDS ANALYSIS

- Key needs include XXXX.

ECONOMIC ANALYSIS

- Key points include XXXX.

FINAL THOUGHTS

You now have all the tools you need to create lots of fuzzy ideas and turn one into a clear product or service. You are ready to GO BIG! The creative mindset creates the spark, improvisation fuels the flames and design thinking focuses the energy. The toolkit provides a concise checklist and templates to get things done.

Like most things in life, the creative mindset must be practiced daily to improve. In time, doors of possibility, or new ideas, will present themselves with less effort. Develop habits that enhance your expertise, promote divergent thinking, seek new stimulus and commit to physical activities that require both low and high intensity thinking. Use the tools of a Cool Products list and "What makes me frustrated" list, Idea Sketch and "Imagine in 5 years…"

Creativity is often messy with changes in direction. With more practice, you will develop more confidence that you will find a creative outcome. Optimize your own creative mindset by experimenting with different habits.

Take advantage of creating in teams. Group improvisation usually leads to a faster recognition of a changed reality and effective outcomes. Improvisation can help to connect the dots more quickly. This outcome is achieved by having a team comprised of people with different skillsets and perspectives. The challenge is to quickly establish the mutual respect of group members by developing authentic relationships. Use the group exercises, as well as the rules of ideation and editing. This trust leads to great team chemistry, which can help get you past setbacks and different personal differences. The result is often outstanding outcomes.

Use design thinking as a problem solving process of channeling creativity to identify problems and create solutions. The method is based on repeated improvements based on research and ideation from a diverse design team. The goal is a clear product /service specification which has been vetted through repeated interactions with users and stakeholders. The PRICE method was created to make it easier to remember the process: Problem, Research, Ideation, Curation and Edit.

Utilize the Toolkit to help guide you through the creativity and Design Thinking process with checklists and templates.

In this book we have discussed the essentials of a creative mindset, improvisation, design thinking, and the toolkit. The next step is to use the process several times and develop your own creative process. Live the innovative life. GO BIG!

www.ingramcontent.com/pod-product-compliance
Lightning Source LLC
Chambersburg PA
CBHW081137170526

45165CB00008B/2706